When Kids Don't Know the Basics

Paul Borthwick
Randy Southern
Steve Hickey
Tim Richards
Mike Hilton
Robert Ayres

David C. Cook Publishing Co. Elgin, Illinois—Weston, Ontario

First Aid for Youth Groups
When Kids Don't Know the Basics

© 1992 David C. Cook Publishing Co.

Scripture quotations are from the *Holy Bible, New International Version* (NIV), © 1973, 1978, 1984 by the International Bible Society. Used by permission of Zondervan Bible Publishers.

Published by
David C. Cook Publishing Co.
850 N. Grove Ave., Elgin, IL 60120
Cable address: DCCOOK
Illustrations by Bill Duca
Design by Sandi Welch and Randy Maid
Printed in U.S.A.

ISBN: 1-55513-510-2

FirstAid
FOR YOUTH GROUPS

When Kids Don't Know the Basics

ABOUT THE AUTHORS

Paul Borthwick is Minister of Missions at Grace Chapel in Lexington, Massachusetts. A former youth pastor and frequent speaker to youth workers, he is the author of several books, including *Organizing Your Youth Ministry* and *Feeding Your Forgotten Soul: Spiritual Growth for Youth Workers* (Zondervan).
Paul wrote the "Helping the Biblically Illiterate" article for this book.

Randy Southern is an editor in the Church Services division of David C. Cook. He has also written several books, including *It Came from the Media* and *Cross Training* (SonPower).
Randy wrote sessions 1-4 of this book.

Steve Hickey served for several years as the junior high minister at Hillcrest Covenant Church in Kansas City. He is studying at North Park Theological Seminary in Chicago.
Steve wrote sessions 5-6 of this book.

Tim Richards, a former junior high director and high school youth pastor, is currently pastor of adult ministries at the Sierra Bible Church in Sonora, California. He is also a free-lance curriculum writer.
Tim wrote sessions 7-8 of this book.

Mike Hilton is director of Christian education at the Tabernacle Church of Norfolk, Virginia. In his eleven years of Christian education experience, he has also served as youth pastor, summer camp director, and retreat coordinator.
Mike wrote sessions 9-10 of this book.

Robert Ayres is director of the Christian Education Center and Adolescent Counseling Center in Gainesville, Georgia. He's been involved in youth ministry for over fifteen years.
Robert wrote sessions 11-15 of this book.

DOES YOUR GROUP NEED FIRST AID?

Wise is the youth worker who heeds this rule: "Expect the unexpected."

Whether they're as personal as a relationship breakup or as universal as a question about God's nature . . . whether they involve a debate about R-rated movies or an incident of racial division . . . problems, questions, attitudes, and situations will arise that disrupt the life of your group.

Is it really possible to prepare for such disruptions? Now it is—with "First Aid for Youth Groups."

Each book in the "First Aid for Youth Groups" series is designed to help you respond quickly to specific issues, situations, and events that affect your group.

With the practical, biblical advice contained in each session, you'll be able to help your group members understand such basic faith issues as what the Holy Spirit does, why we need the Bible, and how Christianity differs from other religions. You'll be ready to respond to group members' questions as to whether it's wrong to date non-Christians or why Christians "never seem to have any fun." You'll be prepared to deal with specific obstacles that prevent your group from experiencing true fellowship. And you'll be able to help group members address such personal hurts as problems in school and family disgrace.

Created with the help of veteran youth workers, these sessions do more than address the problems and situations affecting individuals in your group. They're also designed to raise the sensitivity of other group members, and cause the group itself to be an instrument of healing.

No one can solve serious problems with a meeting or two. But with "First Aid for Youth Groups," you can be ready with immediate help when symptoms appear. The prescription: Pick sessions as needed and apply the wisdom of God's Word directly to your group.

— **Randy Southern, Series Editor**

HELPING THE BIBLICALLY ILLITERATE

Illiterate: "Showing or marked by a lack of acquaintance with the fundamentals of a particular field of knowledge" (*Webster's Ninth New Collegiate Dictionary*).

Many of the kids we are trying to reach are illiterate when it comes to the doctrines of Christianity. Some do not know who came first—Abraham, Jesus, or Moses—or whether they were contemporaries ("Wasn't Moses one of the twelve—or was it ten—disciples?"). Others think that "Christ" is Jesus' last name.

Our church youth may be only a few steps ahead of their unchurched counterparts. Kids today think the "Great Commission" comes after a great sale, that John 3:16 is a sign to be held up at athletic events, and that the Ten Commandments were given to Charlton Heston on the top of Mount Sinus.

The "Peanuts" comic strip illustrated Christian illiteracy in a strip in which Lucy was writing a paper on church history. In the first panel she writes, "To understand church history, we must go back to the very beginning." Then she continues: "Our pastor was born in 1948."

With biblical ignorance and Christian illiteracy on the increase, how can we respond? The sessions that follow give practical handles for addressing the basics of Christian faith and doctrine; but before proceeding, consider several foundational attitudes and facts that can provide a strong base on which to build.

Self-Examination

Sometimes kids demonstrate a fuzziness about Christian truth because we who teach are fuzzy in our own beliefs. *Evangelicalism*, a study by James Davidson Hunter, revealed that many students in conservative Christian colleges across the country are unclear in their beliefs about hell and the fate of those without Christ.

Here's one of the reasons why: Students lack convictions about these issues because they came from churches that did not preach convictions, and because they study under professors who appear wishy-washy on the issue. In a world besieged by pluralistic thinking, even Christian leaders hesitate to say boldly, "No one comes to the Father but by Jesus" (see John 14:6) or "There is salvation in no one else" (see Acts 4:12).

Therefore, before we address questions like "Who is Jesus?" or "How is Christianity different from other religions?" we'd better ask ourselves, "What do *I* believe about these topics?"

Doctrines That Matter

In the pragmatic world of youth ministry, we find it easy to look for the fastest answers to crisis questions. Therefore, issues like "Why is the church important?" or "What is the Old Testament all about?" do not compel us.

As a youth worker, it's much easier for me to spend five weeks dealing with questions about sex and dating than one week explaining the Holy Spirit. Motivation intensifies for the first issue and disappears for the second.

But sending dozens of students off to secular colleges has rebuked my nonchalance toward the Christian "basics." Students who have gone to secular colleges or universities without a basic understanding of Christian doctrine have been the most susceptible to losing their faith in philosophy class or falling prey to the biblical manipulations of cults.

No matter how strong their moral convictions are, if kids do not link their morality with biblical underpinnings, Christianity becomes just one more contribution to "values formation." Therefore, teaching the "basics" in the youth group provides kids with essential training for future challenges to their faith.

The Dangers of a Superior or Intolerant Attitude

Even though we want to demonstrate our own convictions, we must avoid a superior attitude that conveys intolerance. A new group member asked me a question about "Adam on the ark." I tried gently to explain the error rather than ridiculing the biblical illiteracy of the question. Ridicule will guarantee only one thing: that the kid will never ask another question.

One difficulty we face is fostering this tolerance in the group members who *do* know the biblical facts. Helping kids who have completed fourteen years of Sunday school (or who attend the local Christian school) to reach out to the biblically illiterate—without ridiculing their questions—is part of our challenge.

New Christians coming to us today have images of God that combine the "Force" from *Star Wars* with New Age concepts and emotional images created by their own fathers. As a result, their questions about the character of God may reflect a total lack of biblical information. We must listen carefully so that we understand their misconceptions before we correct them by teaching the truth.

A Reflection of Their Parents

The Christian education of young people is part of a bigger picture. Christian kids who demonstrate biblical ignorance tell us something about the biblical knowledge of their parents. Many parents (even in the church) do not know much more about the Trinity, church history, or the Old Testament than their children do!

A father once told me that he thought the "Great Commission" was 15 percent. Another parent critiqued our program by asking, "Do you always have to emphasize the Bible? Can't you just focus on having *fun*?" Questions like these reveal the viewpoints and values being communicated at home.

Our efforts to teach kids the "basics" function best as part of an overall church commitment to educate adults in these same "basics." Christian kids are more likely to grow, study the Bible, and pray if they see adults doing the same.

Explaining Terms

We can't assume that new Christians understand the concepts that we in "church culture" know well. Unchurched kids and new Christians will not be familiar with words like "blessed" or "holy."

But in addition to avoiding Christian jargon, we also need to define basic terms like God, prayer, and Christian. Even the biblical definition of sin needs elaboration. One group member limited sin to "those acts that hurt others"; by his definition, sin included murder, robbing (from the poor, but not the rich), and rape. Lust, drunkenness (as long as you don't drive), and cheating on exams came under the category of acceptable behavior. Without expanding his definition according to what the Bible says, he might never see himself as a sinner.

Discipleship Today

Two new Christians in the youth group looked ready for our leadership team. They were enthusiastic about their faith and anxious to grow. Just before recruiting them to leadership, however, we found out that they were both sexually active and that their fellow group members knew it.

We confronted them with the issue, and each one gave the same response: "It never occurred to us that it was wrong." Their secularized upbringing, combined with permissive parents, yielded behavior that contrasted with biblical standards of purity.

The experience reminded us that discipleship today takes time, teaching, and relationship-building. We cannot assume that new Christians have any of the Christian foundations that we might have assumed fifteen years ago. The "post-Christian" generation has arrived.

As followers of Jesus Christ, we believe in His truth and its application to daily living. We believe we are the children of light working in our world to dispel darkness. Now the challenge is to put this belief into practice with the young Christians that Jesus has given us.

— **Paul Borthwick**

Session 1

If asked, most young people would probably have no problem admitting that they believe in God. However, ask them to explain what they believe *about* God and their answers might not be so readily available.

We're familiar with the various stereotypes of God: the cosmic "spoilsport," out to destroy people's fun; the loving old man who sits in His heavenly rocking chair, watching the sins of the world and shrugging His shoulders as if to say, "Oh well, humans will be humans"; the celestial gift-giver, ready to bestow all kinds of fabulous presents on us, if we only ask Him to; the vengeful dictator, who enjoys nothing more than wiping out entire armies or towns; etc.

These stereotypes are the result of ignorance of God's true character. It's important that young people understand the nature and attributes of God—after all, is it possible to have a personal relationship with someone when you don't even know what the person is like?

Rather than doing a quick summary of the dozens of God's attributes, this session narrows the focus to four: His omniscience, His omnipotence, His holiness, and His love. Not only will your young people discover what these attributes involve, but they'll also understand what the attributes have to do with their lives.

What Is God Like?

Specific Aims
• To help group members understand the following perfections of God: His omniscience, omnipotence, holiness, and love; and to help kids understand what God's perfections have to do with their lives.

Scriptural Support
• Exodus 3:13, 14
• Psalms 5:5; 139:1-16, 23, 24
• Jeremiah 31:3
• Habakkuk 1:13a
• Romans 5:6-8
• Colossians 1:16
• I John 1:5; 4:9, 10

Special Preparation
• Bibles
• Copies of Student Sheet 1-A ("I Am Sends Me")
• Copies of Student Sheet 1-B ("Because God Is, I Can . . .")
• Pencils
• Chalkboard and chalk or newsprint and marker
• Paper
• Index cards
• Art supplies (colored paper, scissors, glue, markers, etc.)

1 I Am

Open the session with an activity designed to get group members thinking about who God is. Distribute paper and pencils. Instruct each group member to describe himself or herself by completing the phrase "I am . . ." in five different ways. The descriptions shouldn't be too obvious or personal, however. When everyone is finished, you will collect the sheets and read each one aloud while the rest of the group members guess whose it is.

A sample description sheet might include the following:

"I am . . .
- originally from Indiana;
- part Irish and part Italian;
- a Chicago Cubs fan;
- interested in photography;
- allergic to peanut butter."

After you've read through the group members' descriptions, say something like: **There's one more description I'd like to read to you. See if you can guess who fits this description: "I Am."** When your group members ask you to complete the statement, have someone read aloud Exodus 3:13, 14.

Ask for three volunteers to perform a quick skit. Distribute a copy of Student Sheet 1-A ("I Am Sends Me") to each volunteer. Send the three actors out of the room for a few minutes to prepare.

When they're gone, say something like: **Imagine that you're one of the Israelites. Some guy named Moses comes to you and says that "I Am" sent him. How would you respond to him? What questions might you ask him?**

After a few group members respond, bring in your actors to perform the skit. When they're finished, give them a round of applause.

Ask: **If you were going to tell someone about God, how would you describe Him?** Supplement group members' responses with the following: holy, omnipresent (exists everywhere, all the time), omniscient (all-knowing), omnipotent (all-powerful), loving, merciful, sovereign, and eternal. Write the descriptive words and phrases on the board as they are named.

Announce that while all of God's attributes are important, you want to concentrate specifically on four of them: His omniscience, His omnipotence, His holiness, and His love.

2 God's "Omni-" Attributes

Before the session, you will need to talk to the parents of at least three of your group members. Ask the parents to supply you with personal—but not embarrassing or threatening—information regarding their kids. The information should include "cute" things the kids did when they were babies, nicknames given to the kids by their families, and the names of any pets the kids had when they were very young. However, group members must not know that you've been talking to their parents.

Distribute index cards and pencils. Say something like: **For this next activity, I'll need to get some personal information from you. Write on your index cards the answers to these three questions:**

(1) What was the cutest thing you ever did when you were a baby?

(2) What nickname did your family give you?

(3) What was the name of the first pet you ever had? What kind of animal was it?

When group members are finished, ask volunteers to share their responses. As much as possible, work in the information you obtained earlier from group members' parents. For instance, you might say something like: **Judy, I think the cutest thing you ever did was when you put that ice-cream cone in your hair at the mall. I'll never forget the way you looked, with the chocolate ice cream running down your face.** Or you might say something like: **Skeeter—I mean, Mark—what nickname did your family give you?** Or you might ask: **Andrea, did you get your cocker spaniel before or after Harry, your hamster, died?**

When kids ask how you know so much about them, act as though you know *all* about their personal lives. Then, after a minute or two, explain how you got the information.

Ask: **How would you feel if you found out that there was a person who knew about everything you've ever done and every thought you've ever had?** (Ashamed, embarrassed, as though your privacy had been invaded.)

Circle the word "omniscient" on the board. Then have volunteers read aloud Psalm 139:1-16, 23, 24. Ask: **How does God's omniscience, or "all-knowingness," relate to us?** (He perceives our thoughts; He knows what we're going to say even before we do; He knows exactly what's going to happen in our lives; etc.)

According to this psalm, *how* does God know us so well? (He created us.)

How might God's knowledge of our thoughts, actions, and lives be beneficial to us? (We can go to Him with questions about what we should do; reminding ourselves that God knows what we're doing and thinking can keep us from getting ourselves into trouble.)

What might be some possible "drawbacks" of God's knowing everything about us? (He knows when we do something wrong; we may have the feeling that we're being "watched" all the time.)

Have group members form pairs. Distribute art supplies (colored paper, scissors, glue, markers, etc.) to each pair. Instruct the pairs to create the "ultimate comic book superhero." They should design the superhero's costume and list his or her powers and abilities.

Encourage the pairs to be creative in their designs. Give them several minutes to work; then have them share and explain their creations.

Say something like: **These superheroes and their powers are products of our imaginations.** Circle the word "omnipotent" on the board. **But when we're talking about the power of God, we're talking about something *beyond* our imaginations.**

When we say that God is omnipotent, or "all-powerful," what do we mean? Encourage a couple of volunteers to respond.

Have someone read aloud Colossians 1:16. Then ask: **According to this verse, what things in the world are the result of God's creation?** (Everything.)

If God created everything in the world, what does that tell you about His power over worldly things? (A creation cannot be greater than its creator. Therefore, God has total power over every aspect of the world.)

Besides Creation, what other biblical examples can you think of in which God demonstrates His power? Supplement group members' responses with the following suggestions: the destruction of Sodom and Gomorrah; the destruction of the entire population, except for Noah and his family, with the great Flood; the parting of the Red Sea for Moses and the Israelites; the protection of Shadrach, Meshach, and Abednego in the fiery furnace; etc.

How do you think most Christians feel about God's power? (Secure; protected; some might even take it for granted.)

How might non-Christians feel about God's power? (Insecure; fearful; some may see only the destructive nature of His power and assume He's an angry God, ready to destroy anything that displeases Him.)

3 HOLY, BUT LOVING

Ask: **Which of the following do you think most closely resembles the way God feels about sin? Why?**
  (a) **The way a little kid feels about a food he or she doesn't like**
  (b) **The way an army drill sergeant feels about his recruits "goofing off"**
  (c) **The way a police officer feels about crime**
  (d) **The way a cancer researcher feels about cigarettes**
  (e) **The way Superman feels about kryptonite**
  (f) **Other** _____

Ask most of your group members to offer their opinions. Encourage them to use their own analogies whenever possible.

Ask: **Why does God feel the way He does about sin?** If no one in the group mentions it, suggest that it's because of His holiness.

What does it mean to be holy? (Morally perfect, pure, completely free of any sin or unrighteousness.)

Have volunteers read aloud Psalm 5:5; Habakkuk 1:13a; and I John 1:5. Then ask: **How does God's holiness affect His attitude toward sin?** (Because He is perfectly holy, God cannot have anything to do with anything that is sinful or unrighteous.)

Say something like: **Let's find out a little more about God's holiness. I need someone to read Jeremiah 31:3.** When your volunteer finishes reading the verse, say: **Wait a minute—that's not right. Are you sure you read that verse correctly? After all, if God is holy and can have nothing to do with sin, how can He say that He *loves* sinful people?** Encourage a few group members to offer their opinions.

How do we *know* that God loves us? Have group members read Romans 5:6-8 and I John 4:9, 10 in response to the question.

How does Jesus' life, death, and resurrection relate to God's holiness *and* His love? (Because of our sin, we have no way to "connect" with God through our own efforts. His holiness demands that all sin be punished. But because God loves us, He sent His Son to the world to take the punishment for *all* sin. Jesus lived a sinless life and took the punishment for our sin; therefore, through Him, we have the opportunity for a relationship with the holy God.)

4 GOD, HIS ATTRIBUTES, AND ME

Distribute copies of Student Sheet 1-B ("Because God Is, I Can . . ."). Give group members a few minutes to fill out the sheets. Announce that their answers are private—no one will be asked to share what he or she wrote.

If you see that group members are having trouble with the sheet, you may want to read the following possible responses to stimulate their thinking.

Omniscient—Areas in which God's guidance is needed might include future plans (college, career choice, etc.), dating life, and relationship with parents; areas of temptation might include sex, drinking, smoking, and gossiping.

Omnipotent—Obstacles or problem areas might include lust/pornography, controlling the tongue (gossiping, swearing, cutting others down), and relationship with parents.

Holy—Areas of sin that we need to learn to hate might include lust/pornography, lying, and drinking or taking drugs.

Loving—People who are difficult to love might include family members, teachers, a former boyfriend or girlfriend, a classmate, or someone at work.

When everyone is finished with the sheet, close in silent prayer, encouraging kids to read through their responses. Challenge kids to take the sheet home and go through it at least once more during the week.

I Am Sends Me

Characters
Moses and two Israelite leaders

Scene
Moses is trying to explain to the Israelite leaders that God, "I Am," has sent him with a message for the Israelites.

LEADER #1: Can I help you?

MOSES: I have a message for the children of Israel.

LEADER #1: I see. And who is this message from?

MOSES: I Am.

LEADER #1: You are . . . what?

MOSES: No, the message is from I Am.

LEADER #2: Wait a minute. Do you have a message?

MOSES: Yes.

LEADER #2: And who's it from?

MOSES: I Am.

LEADER #1: I get it—it's charades! First word sounds like . . .

MOSES: No, *I Am* told me to come.

LEADER #2: That wouldn't be *Sam* I Am, would it?

MOSES *(Impatiently)*: No.

LEADER #1: Sam I Am . . . where have I heard that name before?

LEADER #2: The guy who likes green eggs and ham.

LEADER #1: Oh, yeah. He'd eat them in a box.

LEADER #2: Or with a fox.

MOSES: No, you don't understand.

LEADER #1: Or on a train.

LEADER #2: Or on a plane.

MOSES: Listen to me! I Am—the God of your fathers—has sent me to speak to the Israelites.

LEADER #1 *(Suddenly reverent)*: Oh, *I Am.*

LEADER #2: Well, why didn't you say so in the first place?

BECAUSE GOD IS, I CAN . . .

OMNISCIENT

Lord, because You know everything about my life, You can guide me and help me make difficult decisions. I need Your guidance most right now in these areas:

You also know everything I do, say, and think. Help me to keep this in mind the next time I find myself in a tempting situation. You know that the following things tempt me most:

OMNIPOTENT

Lord, because You are all powerful, I know You can help me overcome any problem or obstacle in my life. Help me to rely on Your power to deal with these problem areas:

HOLY

Lord, because You hate evil, I know I should hate it too. But sometimes doing the wrong thing seems easier or more fun. Help me learn how to hate these sins:

LOVING

Lord, because You love me so much, I know I am supposed to love others. Sometimes that's really hard, and I can't do it on my own. Help me learn how to show more love to the following people:

Lord, I love You, and praise You because You are who You are!

Session 2

"Who is Jesus?" Perhaps no other question is as important as this, because how a person answers will determine his or her entire life outlook. As you address this question with your group members, stress the fact that the question must be answered. You cannot *not* have an opinion. Either you believe that Jesus is who He says He is or you don't.

This session also goes on to stress that, if you believe Jesus is who He says He is, that belief should be evident in the way you live.

WHO IS JESUS?

Specific Aim
• To help group members understand the following roles of Christ: Messiah, Savior, High Priest, and Lord.

Scriptural Support
• Isaiah 9:6, 7; 53:5, 6
• John 8:31
• Acts 8:32-35
• Romans 3:23; 5:8; 6:23
• I Corinthians 10:31
• II Corinthians 5:21
• Hebrews 4:14-16
• I John 2:1

Special Preparation
• Bibles
• Cut-apart copies of Student Sheet 2-A ("Prophecies . . . Fulfilled")
• Copies of Student Sheet 2-B ("Four Choices")
• Pencils
• Chalkboard and chalk or newsprint and marker
• Paper
• Volunteer dressed as described in Step 1

1 THE MESSIAH

Distribute paper and pencils. Instruct group members to come up with some "predictions" regarding this session. They should predict (1) what the topic of this session is; (2) what interruptions—if any—you will experience during the session; and (3) exactly what time the session will end (giving the hour, minute, and second).

After a few volunteers have shared their predictions, share yours. You might say something like: **I predict that the topic of this session is "getting to know Jesus." I predict that we will be interrupted by** (name of an adult in your church), **who will be wearing a Lone Ranger mask and looking for his pet chicken, Fred.** [NOTE: You will need to plan this segment of the session with a volunteer from your church. Instruct him to wear a mask and interrupt the session, looking for his pet chicken, Fred, as soon as you end your predictions. Then have him leave without saying anything else. Adapt this as you choose. It could be Liz, dressed in a football helmet, looking for her pet frog, Barney.] You'll also need to predict an ending time for the session.

Ask: **Wasn't that amazing how accurately I predicted those things? After all, the topic of our session *is* "getting to know Jesus," and I knew exactly what our "guest" was going to do.** Your group members probably won't be impressed.

What if those predictions had been made two thousand years ago? Would you be any more impressed that they came true today? Ask for one or two responses.

Explain that the first aspect of Jesus you're going to be discussing involves predictions that came true after thousands of years. There are over three hundred prophecies about Jesus in the Old Testament.

Form teams of two or three individuals. Give each team a cut-apart copy of Student Sheet 2-A ("Prophecies . . . Fulfilled"). To save time now, you'll need to cut these sheets apart before the session. Notice how the complete sheet spells the words, "The Messiah" down the center. Cut down the middle, and cut along all the dotted lines to separate each New Testament reference. Keep the left half of the sheet with the instructions and the Old Testament verses intact. See which team can be the first to correctly match the verses and spell out the secret message of who Jesus is. The letters in the upper-right corner of the New Testament pieces will help you make sure kids get them back in the right order. The correct answers are: (1) e; (2) g; (3) d; (4) h; (5) f; (6) c; (7) i; (8) j; (9) a; (10) b.

Have someone read aloud Isaiah 9:6, 7. Then ask: **According to this passage, what is the Messiah like?** (A powerful, everlasting, just, righteous ruler.)

Who is the "us" mentioned in verse 6? What people are looking for the Messiah? (The Israelites.)

Explain that the Jewish people in the Old Testament were looking for their Messiah, or "Anointed One," sent from God to save them and establish God's kingdom. The word "Christ" literally means "Messiah." It's not Jesus' last name; it's a title we use to say that He is the Anointed One promised by God throughout the Old Testament.

Ask: **Do you think all these fulfilled prophecies offer enough evidence to conclude that Jesus is the Messiah the Jewish people were looking for? Why or why not?** Encourage several people to respond. Point out, if no one else does, that many Jewish people in Jesus' day didn't believe that He was the Messiah. He didn't fit *their* ideas of what the Messiah would be like and do. This is still true for most Jewish people today. (There are some Messianic Jews who do claim Jesus as the Christ.)

2 WHAT A SAVIOR!

If you have room in your meeting area, play a quick game of "freeze tag." Appoint one person to be the "freezer" and one person to be the "melter." When you say "go," the freezer begins to chase people at random. If a person is tagged by the freezer, that person must remain motionless until touched by the melter. If the melter is tagged by the freezer, no one can be melted. The last person remaining "unfrozen" is the winner.

When everyone is finished, draw an analogy between the game and Jesus' role as Savior. Point out that sin is like the freezer—once we've been touched by it, we're unable to reverse its effects. We need Jesus, the "melter," to save us. (It would probably be wise not to try to stretch the analogy any further than this.)

Write the following Scripture references on the board: Romans 3:23; Romans 5:8; and Romans 6:23. Then form pairs. Instruct the pairs to put the verses into some kind of "logical order." When they're finished, ask volunteers to explain the orders they chose and why. Supplement their suggestions with the following:

(1) Romans 6:23—The result of sin is death.

(2) Romans 3:23—Everyone has sinned and is therefore deserving of death.

(3) Romans 5:8—Despite the fact that everyone deserves death, God has provided us a way to escape death—through the sacrifice of His Son.

Have someone read aloud Isaiah 53:5, 6. Then ask: **Whom is this passage referring to?** (One who would be punished for people's sins.)

What event is this passage referring to? (According to Acts 8:32-35, Jesus' crucifixion.)

What do phrases like "he was pierced" and "he was crushed" tell you about the sacrifice Christ made? (It involved excruciating physical pain.)

Was there any other way for us to avoid the punishment of sin except through Jesus' death and resurrection? If so, how? If not, why not? Discuss this for a few minutes.

Then have someone read aloud II Corinthians 5:21. Explain that Jesus was the only possible person who could bridge the gap sin created between God and man because Jesus was the only person who ever lived without sin. Emphasize the fact that Jesus was not only fully God, but He was also fully man. He had every *opportunity* to sin, just as we do. However, He resisted the temptation to sin throughout His entire life.

3 THE HIGHEST PRIEST

Say something like: **So far we've seen that Jesus is the Messiah promised to the Jewish people, who fulfilled every prophecy concerning the Messiah in the Old Testament. And we've seen that He is the Savior of mankind, who gave His life to restore our relationship with God. Now let's talk about another role of Jesus that affects our lives today.**

Have someone read aloud Hebrews 4:14-16. Then ask: **How is Jesus able to sympathize with our weaknesses?** (He was tempted in the same ways that we are. He experienced the same feelings and emotions we experience.)

Why is it important that Jesus is able to sympathize with our weaknesses? (He knows exactly how to help us in our difficult times.)

What does it mean that Jesus is our "High Priest"? What does He do for us as High Priest? Take a look at I John 2:1. (He speaks to God in our defense when we sin.)

What do you think Jesus might say to God in our defense? (Perhaps He might say, "I have covered over this person's sin with My blood. Do not hold him accountable for it.")

How can we benefit from Jesus' role as High Priest? (Not only can we seek His strength and wisdom when difficult times come, but we can also go to Him in prayer when we sin, asking for His forgiveness.)

4 IS HE LORD?

Point out to your group members that when we talk about the roles of Jesus, we base our information on Scripture in general, and the words of Jesus Himself specifically. Then ask: **How do we know we can really believe that Jesus is who He says He is?**

Distribute copies of Student Sheet 2-B ("Four Choices"). Explain that Jesus must fit into one of these four categories: liar, lunatic, legend, or Lord. Give group members several minutes to complete the sheet; then have volunteers share their responses. If time allows, divide into four groups and have each group try to defend one of the four positions, even if group members don't hold that particular position.

Supplement their answers with the following, as needed.

Liar—The problem with this position is that while many people don't accept Jesus as being the Son of God, almost everyone accepts Him as a great moral teacher. Yet if He lied about the most important part of His teaching—His identity—He could hardly be considered a great moral teacher.

Lunatic—The problem with this position is that Jesus never demonstrated any abnormal behavior or mental imbalance. In fact, He was most composed under pressure, when His very life was on the line.

Legend—The problem with this position is that since none of the first three

Gospels were probably written any later than A.D. 70, contemporaries of Jesus were still alive when His words were being documented; they could have corrected any misquotes that the disciples had come up with.

Lord—This position makes sense because not only did Jesus *claim* to be the Son of God and Messiah, but also His actions and life backed up His words.

If any group members believe that Jesus is a liar, legend, or lunatic, offer to meet with them after the session to discuss their beliefs (in a nonthreatening, nonjudgmental manner).

To those group members who believe that Jesus is Lord, ask: **What should Jesus' being Lord mean to our lives?** Read aloud I Corinthians 10:31 and John 8:31 to give them some ideas. Supplement their responses with suggestions like "We should give Him control of every area of our lives" and "We should study His Word regularly to build our relationship with Him."

Close the session in prayer, thanking God for who Jesus is and asking for help in making Him Lord of every area of our lives.

Prophecies ... Fulfilled

To find out who Jesus is, match each of these Old Testament prophecy passages with the New Testament passage that fulfills it.

____ **1.** "But you, Bethlehem Ephrathah, though you are small among the clans of Judah, out of you will come for me one who will be ruler over Israel, whose origins are from of old, from ancient times" (Micah 5:2).

Matthew 2:1-6

e.

____ **2.** "Therefore the Lord himself will give you a sign: The virgin will be with child and will give birth to a son, and will call him Immanuel" (Isaiah 7:14).

Luke 1:26, 27

g.

____ **3.** "Rejoice greatly, O Daughter of Zion! Shout, Daughter of Jerusalem! See, your king comes to you, righteous and having salvation, gentle and riding on a donkey, on a colt, the foal of a donkey" (Zechariah 9:9).

John 12:12-16

d.

____ **4.** "Even my close friend, whom I trusted, he who shared my bread, has lifted up his heel against me" (Psalm 41:9).

Matthew 26:14-16

h.

____ **5.** "They divide my garments among them and cast lots for my clothing" (Psalm 22:18).

Matthew 27:35

f.

____ **6.** "It must be eaten inside one house; take none of the meat outside the house. Do not break any of the bones" (Exodus 12:46).

John 19:31-36

c.

____ **7.** "All who see me mock me; they hurl insults, shaking their heads: 'He trusts in the Lord; let the Lord rescue him. Let him deliver him, since he delights in him'" (Psalm 22:7, 8).

Luke 23:11

i.

____ **8.** "I will raise up for them a prophet like you from among their brothers; I will put my words in his mouth, and he will tell them everything I command him" (Deuteronomy 18:18).

John 7:14-17

j.

____ **9.** "In the day," declares the Sovereign Lord, "I will make the sun go down at noon and darken the earth in broad daylight" (Amos 8:9).

Matthew 27:45

a.

____ **10.** "Therefore my heart is glad and my tongue rejoices; my body also will rest secure, because you will not abandon me to the grave, nor will you let your Holy One see decay" (Psalm 16:9, 10).

Acts 2:24-27

b.

FOUR CHOICES

When we look at the claims of Christ and the Bible, it becomes clear that we must choose one of four positions regarding Christ. He is either a liar, a lunatic, a legend—or He is Lord. Take a look at the following brief explanations and decide for yourself. As you fill in the blanks, try to offer *logical, factual* information when possible, instead of sharing just your *opinions*.

LIAR

One possibility is that Jesus knew He wasn't the Son of God, the Messiah, or the Savior—but He deliberately lied about those facts to His followers to make His teachings seem more important.

I believe/don't believe that Jesus is a liar because _____

_____

_____

LUNATIC

Another possibility is that Jesus really believed Himself to be who He said He was—but was self-deceived. If this is the case, Jesus was actually an egomaniacal madman who happened to have come up with some pretty profound teachings.

I believe/don't believe that Jesus is a lunatic because _____

_____

_____

LEGEND

Yet another possibility is that Jesus Himself never actually claimed to be the Son of God or the Messiah, but that those words were "put in His mouth" by His overeager disciples. If this is the case, Jesus was merely a great teacher who has been misunderstood by modern Christianity.

I believe/don't believe that Jesus is a legend because _____

_____

_____

Lord

The final option is that Jesus is exactly who He claimed to be: the Son of God, the Messiah, the Savior, the High Priest. If this is the case, then Jesus is deserving of our worship and praise—and control of our lives.

I believe/don't believe that Jesus is Lord because _____

_____

_____

Session 3

We might describe the Holy Spirit as the "unsung" member of the Trinity. Most kids know that God the Father is Creator, that Jesus is the Son and Savior, and that the Holy Spirit is . . . the other Person mentioned during baptismal services.

Chances are that your study of the Holy Spirit will primarily involve connecting Him with functions and areas of the Christian life that your kids are already familiar with—including prayer, Bible study, and spiritual gifts. Once your group members understand the roles of the Holy Spirit, they'll have a better idea of His importance in their lives.

WHAT DOES THE HOLY SPIRIT DO?

Specific Aim

• To help group members understand the following functions of the Holy Spirit: comforting and teaching Christians in a non-Christian world, convicting Christians of their sins, helping Christians direct their prayers, and bestowing spiritual gifts.

Scriptural Support

• John 14:15-20, 25, 26; 16:13-15
• Acts 1:4
• Romans 8:26, 27; 12:6-8
• I Corinthians 2:9, 10; 12:7-11
• Galatians 5:16, 17
• I Thessalonians 1:4, 5

Special Preparation

• Bibles
• Copies of Student Sheet 3-A ("A Jungle Adventure")
• Copies of Student Sheet 3-B ("The Gift That Keeps On Giving")
• Pencils
• Chalkboard and chalk or newsprint and marker
• Slips of paper prepared according to the instructions in Step 3

1 THE COUNSELOR/TEACHER

Before the session, choose four group members to participate in a brief skit. Distribute copies of Student Sheet 3-A ("A Jungle Adventure") to the actors and have them read through the script a couple of times before the session starts. Encourage them to "go overboard" dramatically in their portrayals.

Open the session by having the actors perform the skit (one of them will be responsible for the sound effects). Afterward, lead the rest of the group in a standing ovation.

Say something like: **This skit is an analogy—a way of explaining one thing by using other symbols or objects. For instance, in this analogy, Ron and Heather represent sinful people and the Hero represents Jesus. The jungle represents the world and the tiger represents sin and spiritual death.**

How did Jesus save sinful people? (By giving His life as a sacrifice for our sins.)

What happened after Jesus died for our sins and rose from the dead? (He ascended to heaven.)

How might that be considered similar to what the Hero did in the skit? (It might seem that after Jesus saved us, He left us on our own, forcing us to have to make our way through the world by ourselves.)

Do you believe that Jesus left Christians alone in the world when He ascended to heaven? Why or why not? After a few group members have responded, have a volunteer read aloud John 14:15-20.

Then ask: **Who did Jesus send to be with us when He left?** (The Holy Spirit.)

[NOTE: At this point, it might be a good idea to briefly explain the concept of the Trinity—the Father, Son, and Holy Spirit being three distinct Persons, yet One as a whole. It's important that group members understand that the Holy Spirit is not of any lesser importance or "rank" than God the Father or Jesus, even though His roles may seem subservient.]

Do you "know" the Holy Spirit is living in you, as verse 17 says? If so, how do you know? If not, how do you feel about it? Encourage several group members to respond.

Verse 16 describes the Holy Spirit as the "Counselor." What kind of characteristics does a good counselor have? (Concern for other people, a good listening ability, wisdom, etc.)

When you think of the Holy Spirit as a Counselor, what images do you get of Him? You might want to write group members' responses on the board as they are named.

Ask two volunteers to read aloud John 16:13-15 and I Corinthians 2:9, 10. Then ask: **What roles of the Holy Spirit do these passages describe?** (Guiding us into truth and revealing God's work to us.)

The Bible guides us into truth and explains things God has done. So why do we need the Holy Spirit to do the same thing? If no one mentions it, explain that the Holy Spirit works *with* Scripture. He guides us and reveals God's work to us by helping us apply the principles of Scripture to our individual situations.

2 THE CHRISTIAN'S CONSCIENCE

Write the following passages on the board: John 14:25, 26; Galatians 5:16, 17; and I Thessalonians 1:4, 5. Instruct group members to look up the passages as quickly as possible to discover another role of the Holy Spirit. See if anyone can find something that links these verses together. The answer you're looking for is "The Holy Spirit reminds Christians what is and isn't Christlike behavior."

Ask: **When do you think Christians most need to be reminded what is and isn't Christlike behavior?** If no one mentions it, suggest "when they're being tempted to do something that isn't Christlike."

How does the Holy Spirit remind us of Christlike principles when we can't physically see or hear Him? Encourage several volunteers to offer their opinions.

Then have group members form three teams. Assign each team one of the following case studies. Instruct the teams to brainstorm what methods the Holy Spirit might use in each situation to remind the person of what is and isn't Christlike behavior.

Case Study #1

Jorge is a Christian. One night, Vincent, one of Jorge's friends from school, invited Jorge to go see a movie with him and some other guys from school. Jorge had seen ads for the movie they were going to see, and it looked OK to him; so he agreed. However, when the guys got to the theater, they saw that "Babes on the Beach," an R-rated teen sex comedy, was playing on one of the other screens. After a few minutes of persuading, the rest of the group talked Jorge into going to see "Babes on the Beach."

Case Study #2

Wendy is a Christian, struggling to get through her first semester in college. One night, her roommate Chris came home, triumphantly waving a piece of paper in the air. When Wendy asked her what it was, Chris explained that it was a copy of the biology final exam for which they had both been studying all week. All she would tell Wendy was that "a friend of hers in the biology department had gotten his hands on the test" and given it to her. Excitedly Chris began to read aloud the questions on the test.

Case Study #3

For weeks Max's friends had been talking about how, on Halloween, they were going to get revenge on Mr. Banks, the English teacher, for being so mean. They were planning on vandalizing his house. They all knew that Max is a Christian, so, for the most part, they didn't try to include him in the planning process. However, on the day before Halloween, Mr. Banks accused Max—in front of the whole class—of something Max didn't do. This made Max so angry that after class he asked his friends if he could join them in vandalizing Mr. Banks's house. Of course, they said yes.

After a few minutes, have the teams share what they came up with. Supplement their responses with the following, as needed.

Case Study #1—The Holy Spirit might prompt another Christian in the group to speak up; He might cause Jorge to run into a family from his church, who ask him what he's going to see; He might cause Jorge to feel guilty while watching a steamy sex scene by causing Jorge to remember Christ's words on lust; etc.

Case Study #2—The Holy Spirit might cause Wendy to recall another friend of hers who got caught cheating and had to take a class over again; He might give Wendy the strength to just walk out of the room; etc.

Case Study #3—The Holy Spirit might persuade Max to go to Mr. Banks personally with his anger, rather than vandalizing the man's house; He might cause Max to think about how his actions would affect his witness to his non-Christian friends; etc.

Point out that the Holy Spirit's reminders of Christlike actions and attitudes are not always *preventative*. Sometimes they're designed to make Christians experience guilt for something they've *already* done.

3 THE PRAYER HELPER

For the following activity, you'll need to have several slips of paper, each with one of the following messages written on it:

- "I'm going to walk my dog to the post office and back."
- "I need a new hammer and ladder to fix my roof."
- "I'm happy that my sister returned my jacket to me."
- "I listen to the radio more than I watch TV."
- "My favorite meal is a hamburger and a milk shake."
- "I saw a homeless person living in a box yesterday."
- "My favorite kind of movies are Westerns."
- "I wish I were about a foot taller."
- "I think basketball is more exciting to watch than football."
- "I like the sweater you're wearing."

Have group members form two teams. Announce that you're going to play a game that's a cross between Pictionary and charades. One person from the first team will choose a slip of paper and attempt to get his or her team to guess the message by any means other than talking. He or she may pantomime, draw on the board, point to objects in the room—but may not communicate with words. If his or her team guesses the phrase in one minute, the team receives a point. Teams alternate until all the slips have been used (or until time is up). The team with the most points wins.

Afterward, say something like: **This game demonstrates what it might be like to try to communicate with someone who doesn't understand your language. When government officials go to other countries for meetings, how do they usually overcome language barriers?** (By using a translator.)

Have a volunteer read aloud Romans 8:26, 27. Then ask: **In what ways does the Holy Spirit serve as a "translator" for us?** (When we don't know how to pray or what to pray for, the Holy Spirit translates our confusion into actual prayers to God. He knows what we want to say and says it for us.)

When do we need the Holy Spirit to serve as a translator for us in praying? In what kinds of situations might we not know how to pray or what to pray for?

(When we've sinned and don't know how to ask for forgiveness; when a loved one is suffering with an incurable sickness; when we're unsure about a situation—a potential job, a college choice, etc.)

How is the Holy Spirit able to interpret our prayers when we ourselves don't even know what we want to say? (He knows our hearts, so He has access to the emotions and desires buried so deeply within us that *we* may not even be aware of them.)

How does it feel to know that you have the Holy Spirit as a translator for your prayers? If no one else mentions it, point out that it could remove a lot of pressure—we don't need to be concerned about saying the "right things" in prayer all the time.

4 THE GIFT GIVER

Say something like: **So far, we've seen that the Holy Spirit guides us, reminds us of Christlike actions, and helps us pray. There's one other function He performs that we should know about.**

Ask volunteers to read aloud I Corinthians 12:7-11 and Romans 12:6-8. Then ask: **What function of the Holy Spirit do these passages describe?** (The giving of spiritual gifts to Christians.)

What are spiritual gifts? (Special abilities and/or characteristics given to believers to benefit the body of Christ [all believers].) Try not to get hung up on the specific gifts mentioned in these verses, but be prepared to share your church's views. Rather than focusing on the gifts, draw attention to the Spirit's role in the process.

According to I Corinthians 12:11, what information does the Holy Spirit use in determining what spiritual gift(s) to give to each person? (The verse says that the Holy Spirit gives them "as he determines." The decisions come from His sovereign wisdom, and nowhere else.)

Why is it important to know that our spiritual gifts are given to us by the Holy Spirit? (We know that our spiritual gifts are part of a larger, perfect plan for the entire body of Christ. Knowing that may motivate us to put our gifts to use.)

5 THAT'S THE SPIRIT

Distribute copies of "The Gift That Keeps On Giving" (Student Sheet 3-B) and pencils. As you do, say something like: **In Acts 1:4, before Jesus was taken up to Heaven, He said, "Do not leave Jerusalem, but wait for the gift my Father promised, which you have heard me speak about." He was talking about the Holy Spirit. In what ways is the Holy Spirit a gift? How valuable is this gift to you?**

Give kids a few minutes to work on the sheet individually according to the instructions given. When they're finished, ask volunteers to share their responses. Questions #2 and #3 are probably the least threatening, so start with them. Question #6 is most threatening, so most kids probably won't want to share what they wrote or drew. If kids have difficulty coming up with anything for question #8, have kids suggest gifts and talents they feel others in the group have been given. Encourage those who said "No" or "I'm not sure" on question #1 to talk with you further about what it means to live in the Spirit.

Close the session in prayer, thanking God for the Holy Spirit, and asking Him to make us more aware of the Spirit's role in our lives.

A Jungle Adventure

Setting

As the skit opens, Ron and Heather are making their way through thick brush in the jungle.

Heather: Why did I ever let you talk me into a jungle safari? We could have been in Hawaii right now.

Ron: Yeah, well, if we'd gone to Hawaii, we wouldn't have the opportunity to see all the exotic creatures the brochure promised.

Heather: The only exotic creature we've seen was the spider that crawled up your pant leg. And you didn't seem too happy to see it.
(SOUND EFFECTS: A long, growling sound.)

Ron: Are you hungry again?

Heather: No, why?
(SOUND EFFECTS: Another growl, louder this time.)

Ron: Wasn't that your stomach growling?

Heather: I thought it was you.
(SOUND EFFECTS: Another loud growl.)

Ron: It wasn't me.

Heather: It wasn't me.
(SOUND EFFECTS: Another loud growl.)

Ron: Maybe it was that tiger that's standing right in front of us.
(Heather screams. Just then, "Hero" dramatically enters.)

HERO: Don't be afraid, folks. I know how to handle dangerous situations—I'm a hero.
(Turning in the direction of the tiger) Get out of here! Shoo!
(SOUND EFFECTS: A loud, retreating, whimpering sound.)

Heather *(Turning to Ron)*: He saved us! *(As she talks, "Hero" quickly runs away.)*

Ron: Yes, now maybe he can show us the way out of the jungle!
(Heather and Ron turn, looking for "Hero.")

Heather: He's gone! What kind of hero would save us from a tiger and then leave us on our own, lost in the jungle? *(Ron shrugs.)*

THE GIFT THAT KEEPS ON GIVING

The Holy Spirit is a gift from God. Here are five functions of the Spirit. Look them over, then follow the instructions at the bottom of the page.

Counselor

Gift-giver

Conscience

Prayer-helper

Teacher

1. Have you received the gift of the Holy Spirit?
- [ ] Yes
- [ ] No
- [ ] I'm not sure

2. Put a star inside the box of the function of the Holy Spirit you're most thankful for right now.

3. Put a question mark inside the box of the function of the Holy Spirit you understand the least right now.

4. Inside the Counselor box, write down any questions about your life you'd like to ask the Holy Spirit.

5. Inside the Teacher box, write down some things about God, the Bible, or your faith that you'd like to learn more about.

6. Write down in the Conscience box things you have felt guilty about during the past week. If you don't want to write anything, draw symbols that only you (and God) know the meaning of.

7. In the Prayer-helper box, write down some things you know you should be praying about.

8. In the Gift-giver box, list any gifts, talents, or abilities you feel you've been given. How can you use what you've been given to benefit others?

Session 4

Wait a half hour after eating before you swim. Early to bed, early to rise, makes a man healthy, wealthy, and wise. Feed a cold; starve a fever. Read your Bible. All of these statements are generally accepted to be good advice—in a generic, no-rush kind of way.

Many Christian young people "know" that they should read the Bible because *it's God's Word*. But they're really not sure beyond that what purpose the Bible serves.

This session is designed to help kids recognize the Bible as a tool to discover what God is like and what His will is for our lives.

WHY DO WE NEED THE BIBLE?

Specific Aims

• To help group members understand that the Bible is not an old book that has no bearing on our lives; and to help group members understand that the Bible is the best tool we have available to discover what God is like and what His will is for our lives.

Scriptural Support

- Job 11:7
- Psalm 103:1-18
- Proverbs 2:1-11
- Matthew 9:1-8
- John 15:13
- Romans 5:8
- II Timothy 3:16, 17

Special Preparation

- Bibles
- Copies of Student Sheet 4-A ("Word Association")
- Copies of Student Sheet 4-B ("God's Book at Work")
- Pencils
- Chalkboard and chalk or newsprint and marker
- Paper
- Materials for making bookmarks (see Step 4)

1 REFLEX RESPONSES

Distribute copies of Student Sheet 4-A ("Word Association") and pencils. Instruct group members to complete the sheets, writing down the first word that comes to their minds for each item.

When they're finished, explain that you have a list of sample answers for the sheet. Have group members call out their responses. If a person's response matches the response on your sample list, he or she receives a point. The person with the most points at the end of the game wins.

The sample list is as follows:
1. ice cream (fattening)
2. horror movies (scary)
3. jeans (comfortable)
4. football (violent)
5. romance novels (boring)
6. cigarettes (disgusting)
7. summer (hot)
8. music (loud)
9. Daffy Duck (hilarious)
10. aerobics (healthy)
11. Corvette (fast)
12. beach (crowded)
13. love (mushy)
14. morning (early)
15. the Bible (boring)

Chances are that at least one or two of your group members will use the word "boring" (or some other negative word) to describe the Bible. If not, you should point out that many people—including some Christians—consider the Bible to be boring.

Ask: **What is it about the Bible that causes you (or others) to think of it as being boring?** (Answers might include things like the following: "It's full of words and stories that I don't understand"; "Because it's so ancient, it's like reading a history book"; etc.) Encourage group members to offer their honest opinions.

Without using any clichés or saying something you don't really believe, name three reasons why *you* think the Bible is important. As group members offer suggestions, ask questions to get them to explain their reasoning. For instance, if someone suggests that reading the Bible is important "because it's God's Word," you might ask, "So why is *God's Word* important?" Write group members' suggestions on the board as they are named.

Then say something like: **All of these are good reasons for the Bible's importance; but the one we're going to focus on today is this: The Bible helps us understand what God is like and how He wants to relate to us.**

2 HIGH-SPEED HISTORIES

Have group members form pairs. Set a time limit of one minute for one person in each pair to tell his or her partner as much about himself or herself as he or she can. Instruct the people sharing to talk as fast as possible and relay as much information as possible. Then give a minute for the second person to share.

Afterward, distribute paper. Instruct group members to write as much information about their partners (based *only* on the information their partners shared) as they can remember. The person who remembers the most information about his or her partner wins.

Then say something like: **Imagine that God was your partner for this activity. What kind of information do you think He might share about Himself?** (Answers might include these: "I created the universe"; "I am eternal"; "I sent My Son to save the world"; etc.)

Have someone read aloud Job 11:7. Then ask: **How would you answer these questions? How is it possible for human beings to understand what God is like?** If no one mentions it, suggest that we can understand God only as He takes the initiative in revealing Himself to us.

Have someone read aloud II Timothy 3:16, 17. Then ask: **What does this passage mean when it says, "All Scripture is God-breathed"?** (God was intimately involved in the writing of Scripture. Everything in the Bible came to us from Him.)

We said earlier that the Bible helps us understand what God is like and how He wants to relate to us. Now we see that God Himself is responsible for the Bible. So, in a sense, the Bible is God's way of telling human beings what He's like. What kinds of things does He tell us about Himself? (He is holy and will not tolerate sin; He has complete power over nature; He protects His people; He loves mankind enough to have made the ultimate sacrifice—the death of His Son—to save us; etc.)

Why do you think God wants us to know things like these? (He loves us; He knows that knowing what He's like will be helpful to us.)

3 WHAT'S IN IT FOR YOU?

Say something like: **It's nice to know that God wants us to know what He's like. But is it really that important to us? In other words, what *practical* benefits can we get from reading the Bible?** Encourage several group members to offer their opinions.

Distribute copies of "God's Book at Work" (Student Sheet 4-B). Instruct group members to decide how the Bible might help the kids in the situations. Give them a few minutes to work; then have them share their responses.

Use the following information to supplement group members' answers
Situation #1—If Kim truly understood God's love, she would recognize that

His love is not dependent on anything she does—He loves her exactly as she is. And because He loves her, He will bring people into her life to give her the comfort and support she needs. (Point out that evidence of God's love can be found in John 15:13 and Romans 5:8.)

Situation #2—If Janna truly understood God's forgiveness, she would recognize that when He forgives a sin, He also *forgets* that sin. Knowing that God does not hold her sin against her would help Janna begin to forgive herself and get on with her life. (Point out that evidence of God's forgiveness can be found in Psalm 103:1-18.) [NOTE: In addition to accepting God's forgiveness, Janna also needs to recognize the seriousness of her sin and commit herself to not repeating it.]

Situation #3—If Tim truly understood God's power, he would recognize that God could help him regain the use of his legs at *any* time. He would also recognize that God could supply him with the patience and inner strength to face life as a paraplegic. (Point out that evidence of God's power can be found in Matthew 9:1-8.)

4 BIBLE BLUEPRINTS?

Say something like: **A lot of people talk about wanting to "find God's will for their lives." Do you think that by reading the Bible we can discover what God's will is for us?** Encourage a few group members to respond.

Have someone read aloud Proverbs 2:1-11. Then ask: **What does this passage tell us about finding God's will for our lives?** If no one mentions it, point out that God does not provide a step-by-step blueprint for our lives in His Word. If, however, we continue to learn about Him by reading His Word, we will begin to think as He thinks and make decisions in our lives based on His principles. As we do that, we can be assured that He will guide us in every decision we make.

If time allows, have kids make personalized bookmarks for their Bibles, using markers and construction paper or felt. Instead of writing names on the bookmarks, however, kids should write one or more personal questions they'd really like answered. Encourage them to keep these in their Bibles and to keep looking there for answers. Offer to help kids find pertinent passages after the meeting, if necessary.

Close the session in prayer, thanking God for providing us with the Bible—a tool by which we can discover what He is like and learn His will for our lives.

Word Association

For each of the following items, write down the first word that comes to your mind that describes your feelings about that item.

1. ice cream _____

2. horror movies _____

3. jeans _____

4. football _____

5. romance novels _____

6. cigarettes _____

7. summer _____

8. music _____

9. Daffy Duck _____

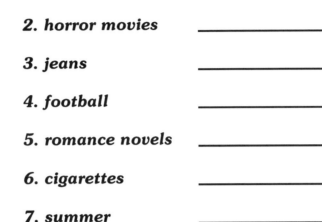

10. aerobics _____

11. Corvette _____

12. beach _____

13. love _____

14. morning _____

15. the Bible _____

GOD'S BOOK AT WORK

Read the following situations. Then write down how the Bible might be helpful to the kids in the situations.

SITUATION #1

Kim's parents were never hesitant to let her know she was a "mistake." Born fifteen years after her sister, Kim always felt like she was an intrusion on her parents' lives. Her parents felt the same way. They never really demonstrated any kind of affection or support toward her, so she grew up thinking that she was unlovable—until she met Alan.

Alan gave her the only love she'd ever experienced. Her entire self-worth was wrapped up in her relationship with him. Yesterday Alan broke up with Kim, saying he didn't love her anymore.

How might reading about God's love in the Bible be helpful to Kim? _____

SITUATION #2

Janna and her boyfriend, Tom, had committed themselves to staying sexually pure until they got married. But one night, in a moment of passion, they broke their commitment. As a result, Janna feels her life is ruined.

Even though she prayed for forgiveness, she still feels terrible. She doesn't want to go to church or youth group because she feels like a hypocrite. She's afraid that everyone will recognize what she's done and think less of her for it.

How might reading about God's forgiveness in the Bible be helpful to Janna? _____

SITUATION #3

When Tim's legs were crushed in a car accident, the doctors told him that he would probably never be able to walk again. But Tim had heard of so many "miraculous recoveries" from such injuries that he paid no attention to the doctors. He committed himself to strenuous physical therapy every day. But now, ten months after the accident, there's still no improvement at all.

When Tim thinks about the prospect of spending the rest of his life as a paraplegic, he gets extremely depressed—and scared.

How might reading about God's power in the Bible be helpful to Tim? _____

Session 5

The children of Israel, trapped between the Red Sea and the Egyptian army, are miraculously rescued when God causes the water in the sea to part, allowing them to walk through on dry land.

David, a teenaged boy carrying only a sling and five stones, defeats Goliath, the heavily armored Philistine giant who has been terrorizing the entire Israelite army.

Jonah, thrown from a ship in the middle of a sea voyage, is swallowed by a great fish. He lives inside the fish for three days, before being "thrown up" on the shore.

The Old Testament is full of interesting stories like these. Chances are that most of your group members are familiar with at least a few such stories. Unfortunately, probably many of your group members know very little else about the Old Testament beyond these stories. To these kids, the Old Testament is irrelevant and even seems to contradict what they know of God in the New Testament.

This session is designed to help your kids understand the Old Testament as a whole. You will help your group members see that the Old Testament records God's efforts to reach people. The Old Testament provides a background for understanding why Jesus came to earth. A closer study of the Old Testament will help us understand more fully who Christ is and what He accomplished.

WHAT IS THE OLD TESTAMENT ALL ABOUT?

Specific Aims
• To help kids understand how the Old Testament fits together as a whole; and to help them recognize that the Old Testament is a record of events leading up to and prophecies concerning the life of Christ.

Scriptural Support
• Psalms 46:1; 119:11
• Proverbs 15:1
• Ecclesiastes 2:10, 11
• Isaiah 9:6, 7; 53:7
• Micah 5:1, 2
• Luke 24:13-35

Special Preparation
• Bibles
• Copies of Student Sheet 5-A ("Old Testament Pie")
• Copies of Student Sheet 5-B ("Jesus B.C.")
• Pencils
• Paper
• Joke books
• Prizes

1 THAT SOUNDS FAMILIAR

Open the session with a "punchline-telling" contest. Ask volunteers to come to the front of the room and tell only the punchlines to their favorite jokes. Emphasize that the punchlines (and the jokes they come from) shouldn't be dirty or offensive. If group members have trouble coming up with punchlines, distribute joke books for them to look through.

After several volunteers have performed, vote as a group on who told the funniest punchline. Award that person a prize.

Hold up a Bible. Suggest that the relationship between the Old Testament and New Testament is similar to the relationship between a joke and its punchline: one can't be fully appreciated without the other.

Have group members form pairs. Distribute paper and pencils to each pair. After you read each of the following clues, give the pairs fifteen seconds to write down their responses.

(1) These two wore the first clothes ever designed. (Adam and Eve—Genesis 3:7.)

(2) He is the most famous shipbuilding zookeeper in the Bible. (Noah—Genesis 6–8.)

(3) He was sold into slavery by his jealous brothers. (Joseph—Genesis 37.)

(4) He talked to a burning bush and had a staff that turned into a snake. (Moses—Exodus 3:1–4:17.)

(5) He received one of the worst haircuts in history. (Samson—Judges 16.)

(6) A giant dressed in full battle armor was no match for this teenager and his sling. (David—I Samuel 17.)

(7) He was thrown into a pit with several hungry lions and emerged the next day unharmed. (Daniel—Daniel 6.)

(8) He spent three days in a "living submarine." (Jonah—Jonah 1–2.)

When the quiz is finished, read the answers and have the pairs grade themselves. Then ask each pair to call out how many correct responses it had. Award prizes to the pair with the *fewest* correct responses.

Say something like: **In case you hadn't noticed, the clues for this quiz were taken from the Old Testament. And even though our "winners" may not have had as many correct responses as the rest of you, they still know more about the Old Testament than most people in our society today.**

On a scale of one to ten, how well would you say you know the Old Testament? Encourage several group members to respond and explain their responses.

Why aren't many people—Christians included—interested in the Old Testament? (It's boring; it doesn't have much to do with our lives today; it's hard to understand what's being talked about when you're not familiar with the culture and practices of that time; etc.)

Say something like: **In this session, we're going to be talking about the Old Testament. Our goal is not necessarily to make you Old Testament scholars, but to help you have a better understanding of what the Old Testament is and why it's important to us today.**

2 OLD TESTAMENT PIE

Explain to your group members that the first step in developing a better understanding of the Old Testament is to identify its three sections.

Distribute copies of Student Sheet 5-A ("Old Testament Pie").

Say something like: **Think of the Old Testament as a pie. There are thirty-nine slices, or books, in the Old Testament pie. The first seventeen slices are** *history* **slices.** Draw group members' attention to the "History" section on Student Sheet 5-A.

Have group members reassemble into the pairs they formed in Step 1. Give the pairs a few minutes to search through the "History" section of the Bible for famous events. Each pair will choose a famous event to act out for the rest of the group. If a pair chooses an event that involves more than two characters, the members of the pair each must play more than one role (using different voices, mannerisms, etc.).

If the pairs have a hard time finding an event to act out, suggest some of the ones listed in the quiz in Step 1.

After all the pairs have performed, ask: **Why is it important for us to know about events that happened thousands of years ago?** If no one mentions it, suggest that these events show us how God relates to and deals with His people. They also provide glimpses of God's awesome power.

Say something like: **The next five slices of the Old Testament pie are** *poetry and wisdom* **slices.** Draw group members' attention to the "Poetry and Wisdom" section on Student Sheet 5-A. **The poetry and wisdom section of the Old Testament contains songs of praise and worship and words of advice on living a godly life.**

Read aloud the following passages (all taken from the poetry and wisdom section of the Old Testament). Have group members suggest ways the principles and advice in each passage might be useful to us today.

• **Psalm 46:1—"God is our refuge and strength, an ever-present help in trouble."** (When we're in trouble, this verse might remind us that we have a place to turn to—a refuge in God, who will keep us safe.)

• **Psalm 119:11—"I have hidden your word in my heart that I might not sin against you."** (Memorizing God's Word—or knowing it well enough to recall it at any time—can help us when we are tempted to sin. God might cause us to remember a passage at a crucial time to prevent us from making a wrong choice.)

• **Proverbs 15:1—"A gentle answer turns away wrath, but a harsh word stirs up anger."** (When we're in conflict with someone, this verse might remind us not to allow the conflict to escalate through harsh words.)

• **Ecclesiastes 2:10, 11—"I denied myself nothing my eyes desired; I refused my heart no pleasure. My heart took delight in all my work, and this was the reward for all my labor. Yet when I surveyed all that my hands had done and what I had toiled to achieve, everything was meaningless, a chasing after the wind; nothing was gained under the sun."** (This passage could serve as a reminder to us that if we spend our time pursuing wealth, fame, and pleasure, ultimately we'll be disappointed by what we attain. We'll realize that our pursuits were meaningless.)

Say something like: **The other seventeen slices of the Old Testament pie are** ***prophecy*** **slices.** Draw group members' attention to the "Prophecy" section on Student Sheet 5-A.

Ask: **What is prophecy?** (Predictions of things that will happen in the future.)

Point out that in addition to other prophecies, the Old Testament contains hundreds of prophecies concerning the Messiah, or Savior.

Ask: **Why do you suppose the Old Testament contains prophecies about the Messiah? Why was it important to know about Him hundreds of years before He came?** If no one mentions it, point out that the prophecies provide signs and "clues" as to what the Messiah would be like and do. As a result, people would be better able to recognize Him when He came.

3 JESUS B.C.

Have group members silently read Luke 24:13-35. Explain that this incident took place just after Jesus' resurrection. Have someone read aloud verse 27.

Ask: **What kinds of things was Jesus explaining to the two on the road to Emmaus?** (He was explaining various Old Testament passages that referred to Him or predicted His coming.) You may want to point out that the only "Scripture" that existed at that time was the Old Testament.

Why was Jesus explaining Old Testament passages to these two? (He was helping them make the connection between the predictions of the Old Testament and the events of His life.)

Distribute copies of Student Sheet 5-B ("Jesus B.C.") and pencils.

Say something like: **The Bible doesn't say exactly what Scripture passages Jesus talked about with the two. Imagine that He talked about the three passages listed on this sheet. How might He have explained each of them to the travelers?**

Give group members a few minutes to work; then have volunteers share their responses. Use the following information to supplement group members' answers.

• *Isaiah 9:6, 7—Jesus may have referred to this passage and said . . .* (When the prophet Isaiah talked about the future of God's people, he said a child would be born who would establish a kingdom that will never end. The child he referred to is Me; the kingdom he described is Mine. You can be a part of My kingdom by following Me.)

• *Micah 5:1, 2—Jesus may have referred to this passage and said . . .* (Micah predicted that from the town of Bethlehem the ruler of Israel would emerge—a ruler who existed from ancient times. I was born in Bethlehem—I am the ruler Micah predicted.)

• *Isaiah 53:7—Jesus may have referred to this passage and said . . .* (Isaiah spoke of one who was led like a lamb to the slaughter and yet remained silent. When I was on trial before the chief priests and Pilate, I remained silent. Later I was led to my crucifixion in the same way a lamb is led to the slaughter.)

Ask: **If Jesus has already fulfilled the prophecies of the Old Testament concerning the Messiah, why is it important for us to know about those prophecies?** If no one mentions it, suggest that we can't *fully* understand who Jesus is and what He's done for us unless we know about the Old Testament prophecies He's fulfilled.

Refer back to some of the events group members acted out in Step 2. Suggest that not only does the Old Testament help us know Christ better, it also contains interesting stories that we might want to read "just for the fun of it."

4 OLD TESTAMENT HURDLES

Wrap up the session with one or more of the following situations, depending on how much time you have left. Each situation presents a different dilemma that will require group members to think through what they've learned about the Old Testament in this session.

After you read aloud a situation, encourage several group members to respond to the questions that follow. Use the information in parentheses to supplement group members' responses.

Situation #1

Last night at youth group, Tom said some things about the Bible that stirred up the rest of the group. Among other things, he said, "The New Testament tells us all we need to know about the Christian life. The Gospels tell the story of Jesus' life and the rest of the books tell us how to live as Christians. So we don't really need the Old Testament anymore. I think Bible publishers should make less expensive Bibles by just using the New Testament." How would you respond to Tom? (The Gospels may tell the story of Jesus' life and work, but to fully appreciate who Jesus is, you must know about the Old Testament prophecies He fulfills.)

Situation #2

Jim, a good friend of yours, is Jewish. He doesn't believe that Jesus is the Messiah predicted in the Old Testament. One day he overhears you talking about the parting of the Red Sea. He is surprised that you know about the incident since you aren't Jewish. You explain to him that the Old Testament in the Bible includes the same books as his Scriptures. The only difference is that the Bible Christians use also includes the New Testament. He asks you how Christians can include the New Testament—which deals with Jesus—with the Old Testament Scriptures. How do you respond? (You could show Jim some of the prophecies concerning the Messiah that Jesus fulfilled. Then you could point out that since Jesus is the Messiah, the New Testament is just as valid as the Old Testament.)

Situation #3

Mary became a Christian at the spring retreat. The speaker said it was important for her to read the Bible so she could grow in her faith and understand more about God. Mary has always loved to read, so this idea seemed easy to her. Several months later, you ask her how her Bible reading is going. She tells

you that she gave up after trying to read the Bible straight through. "The Book of Genesis was OK," she says. "But after that, it was really boring—nothing but a bunch of measurements and family histories." How would you respond to Mary? What parts of the Old Testament might you direct her to? Why? (Explain to her that while *all* of the Bible is important, reading it straight through is not necessarily a good way to study. Suggest that she begin studying more "accessible" Old Testament books like Psalms or Proverbs.)

Close the session in prayer.

OLD TESTAMENT PIE

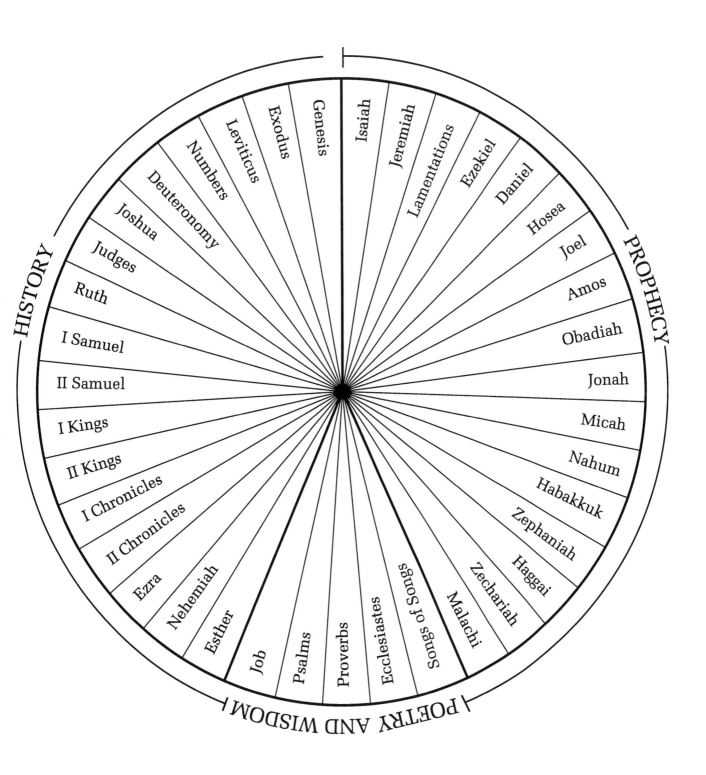

JESUS B.C.

After His resurrection, Jesus appeared to two travelers on the road to Emmaus. They didn't recognize Him. But He revealed Himself to them by explaining what was said in the Old Testament concerning Himself.

The Bible doesn't say which Old Testament passages Jesus explained. Imagine that He talked about the three passages that follow. What might He have said about each one?

ISAIAH 9:6, 7

Jesus may have referred to this passage and said . . .

MICAH 5:1, 2

Jesus may have referred to this passage and said . . .

ISAIAH 53:7

Jesus may have referred to this passage and said . . .

Session 6

It's interesting to read about Jesus' life—but do we really need four books in a row about it?

Does it make any difference today (other than for historians) how the church got started?

The letters of Paul, James, Peter, John, Jude, etc., were written to address the problems and situations of people two thousand years ago. How can they still be applicable today?

What in the world is the Book of Revelation talking about?

Maybe your group members haven't asked these questions in this way, but probably some of your kids have at least wondered about them. This session is designed to provide your group members with an overview of the New Testament. Its purpose is to help your kids understand how books written twenty centuries ago can still have a life-changing impact on us today.

WHAT IS THE NEW TESTAMENT ALL ABOUT?

Specific Aim

• To help kids understand that the New Testament is an eyewitness account of the life of Christ and an instruction manual for us on how to live the Christian life.

Scriptural Support

• Matthew 21:12, 13
• Mark 11:15-17
• Luke 19:45, 46
• John 2:13-21
• Acts 2:42-47
• Romans 3:23; 6:23
• Ephesians 6:1
• Philippians 4:8, 13
• Hebrews 11:1
• James 1:22
• I John 1:9
• Revelation 20:1-10; 21—22

Special Preparation

• Bibles
• Copies of Student Sheet 6-A ("Four Accounts")
• Copies of Student Sheet 6-B ("The Epistle Quiz")
• Pencils
• Chalkboard and chalk or newsprint and marker
• Paper
• Index cards prepared according to the instructions in Step 4
• Prizes
• TV, VCR, and videotape (see Step 1) (optional)

1 EYEWITNESSES

Open the session with an informal discussion time. Ask some of your group members what they've been doing lately, how school is going, what their plans are for later in the week, etc. Then talk for a few minutes about any topic. When you're finished, have group members pair up. Distribute paper and pencils to each pair.

Say: **We're going to have a contest to see how observant you are. With your partner, write down everything that's happened in this meeting so far. Be specific and detailed in your descriptions. I want to know what happened first, what happened second, and so on. As much as possible, use exact quotes. What questions did I ask? How did people respond? What movements did I make? What was going on in the group while we talked?**

Give the pairs a few minutes to work. As they work, you might want to write an account of your own. When everyone is finished, have each pair read its account. Compare and contrast the different accounts. As a group, try to piece together exactly what happened.

[OPTION: You'll need a TV, VCR, and a show you've recorded on videotape. When group members arrive, play a five-minute segment of the show (which you've screened beforehand). Then have group members form pairs. Distribute paper and pencils. Instruct the pairs to write down everything that happened in the segment you just watched. Encourage them to be as detailed as possible in their descriptions. After a few minutes, have each pair share its description. Then replay the segment and see which pair's description was most accurate.]

Ask: **If we were to write a book that described the day-to-day things that happen in this group, how many people do you think would want to read the book?** (Not very many.) **Why?** (The day-to-day things that happen in the group probably aren't that exciting and don't really affect many people outside the group. Therefore, they would be of little interest to most people outside the group.)

Hold up a Bible open to the New Testament. Say: **The first four books of the New Testament all describe the day-to-day events in the life of one man. And yet, *millions* of people have read the New Testament. Why would people be interested in reading something like that?** (The man whose life is described is Jesus Christ. The day-to-day events that are described changed the world.)

2 FOUR ACCOUNTS

Explain that the first four books of the New Testament—the Gospels of Matthew, Mark, Luke, and John—describe Jesus' birth, life, death, resurrection, and ascension. Among the events covered in these books are Christ's miracles, His sermons, His relationship with His disciples and other followers, His attitude and actions toward those who didn't believe in Him, His care and compassion for the disabled and needy, etc.

Say: **Matthew and John were disciples of Christ—they were with Him day and night throughout His entire ministry. Mark wasn't a disciple—but tradition tells us that most of the information in his book came from Peter, who was one of Jesus' best friends. Luke wasn't a disciple, either—but tradition tells us that he got most of the information in his book through interviews and discussions with eyewitnesses. What does this tell you about the events described in the Gospels?** (The accounts can be expected to be reliable since they come from people who witnessed the events firsthand.) You'll want to mention that *all* of the Bible authors were guided in their writing by the Holy Spirit; but avoid getting into a lengthy discussion of inspiration.

Say: **When we tried to describe what happened in the first few minutes of this session, our accounts were somewhat different. How well do you think the accounts of the four Gospel writers "match up"? After all, the books were written at different times, in different places, and under different circumstances.** Encourage a couple of group members to offer their opinions.

Distribute copies of Student Sheet 6-A ("Four Accounts"). Give group members a chance to read the four different accounts of Jesus' clearing the temple.

Then ask: **How do these accounts differ?** (John's account elaborates more on the details of the incident; the wording of the other three accounts differs slightly.) Point out that none of the accounts contradicts the others. The basic facts are the same in each one. Suggest that this lends credibility to the truthfulness and accuracy of the Gospels. (NOTE: Many Bible scholars assume John's account refers to an earlier temple scene, because of where it is placed.)

To give group members an idea of what kinds of things are covered in the Gospels, play a quick game. Have group members reassemble into the pairs they formed earlier. Make sure that each pair has a Bible and that each pair knows where the Gospels are found in it.

One at a time, read aloud the following events found in the Gospels. The pairs will then try to find a reference in which each event is described. When a pair finds a reference, one of the members will run to the board and write it down. For instance, if you asked for "Jesus performing a miracle," a pair might write down "John 2:1-11" (turning the water to wine). The first pair to write down a correct reference gets a point. The pair with the most points at the end of the game wins.

Here are some of the events you might use:
• Jesus' birth
• Jesus performing a miracle
• Jesus using a parable or story to make a point
• Jesus calling His disciples
• Jesus' crucifixion
• Jesus' resurrection

Afterward, ask: **Why are the Gospels important?** If no one mentions it, point out that the events and truths contained in the Gospels are the basis of our entire faith. If we don't believe the Gospels' account of what Jesus did, there's no reason to be a Christian.

3 THE LITTLE CHURCH THAT COULD

Say: **After Jesus died and was resurrected, He ascended back to heaven. But before He left, He promised that one day He would return to earth. How do you think His followers felt after Jesus had gone back to heaven?** (Scared, anxious for Him to return, unsure about what to do, lonely, etc.)

Say: **Sometime after Jesus' death, the Roman government was eager to wipe out Christianity completely. So not only did Jesus' followers have to deal with the physical absence of their leader, but they also had to deal with the threat of death because of their faith.**

What would you have done if you had been one of Jesus' followers during this time? Point out that the first-century Christians banded together in fellowship to support and encourage each other. They formed the early church.

Explain that the Book of Acts, written by Luke, describes the early Christians—their lifestyles, fellowship habits, methods for spreading the news about Christ, etc.

Have someone read aloud Acts 2:42-47.

Ask: **According to this passage, how did the early Christians spend their time?** (Listening to the apostles' teaching, fellowshipping together, praying, spending time with one another, meeting together to worship God, spreading the news of Christ to others, etc.)

Point out that the Book of Acts also describes in detail the ministries of Peter and Paul—two of the most important figures in the history of Christianity.

Why is the Book of Acts important? (From a historical standpoint, it tells us about the "early days" of Christianity—how the news of Christ spread and how the church developed. Also, many of our church traditions today can be traced back to the practices of the early believers.)

4 OTHER PEOPLE'S MAIL

Before the session, you'll need to prepare several index cards. On three of the cards, write "You win!" On the rest of the cards, draw a big "X." Hide the cards around the room.

At this point in the session, explain that you're going to have an instruction-following contest. You will be giving instructions on how to find the various cards ("From the wastebasket, take three big steps toward the door, turn right, and look under the rug").

The object of the game is to choose the proper instructions to follow. If a group member finds a card with an "X" on it, he or she is out of the game. If a group member finds a card with "You win!" on it, he or she wins a prize.

Say something like: **Some of the early Christians faced similar problems. They too didn't know whose instructions to follow. Due to the efforts of the early church, many people became Christians—people who had not heard Christ** speak in person. These new Christians didn't have a complete understanding of what Christ taught. As a result, some of them began introducing ideas from other religions and cults into Christian teachings.

Christian leaders began writing letters to various churches, reinforcing Christ's teachings and giving instructions on how to apply those teachings to everyday life.

These letters were known as "epistles." Twenty-one of these epistles are included in the New Testament. Let's take a quick quiz to see how much you know about the epistles.

Distribute copies of Student Sheet 6-B ("The Epistle Quiz") and pencils. Give group members a few minutes to work. Then go over the answers as a group.

The answers are as follows:

(1) Galatians
(2) Colossians
(3) II Thessalonians
(4) II Timothy
(5) Philemon
(6) I Corinthians
(7) I John
(8) I Thessalonians
(9) Hebrews
(10) Philippians
(11) II Peter
(12) Romans
(13) II John
(14) James
(15) Titus
(16) III John
(17) I Peter
(18) Jude
(19) Ephesians
(20) I Timothy
(21) II Corinthians

Ask: **If these letters were written to first-century Christians, why are they important to us today?** (They contain principles that are as applicable to our lives today as they were to the lives of first-century Christians.)

To give your group members an idea of some of the "famous" principles found in the epistles, read aloud the following passages. (Depending on how well your group members know the passages, you may want to read just part of each one and ask volunteers to complete it.)

• **"For all have sinned and fall short of the glory of God"** (Romans 3:23).

• **"For the wages of sin is death, but the gift of God is eternal life in Christ Jesus our Lord"** (Romans 6:23).

• **"Children, obey your parents in the Lord, for this is right"** (Ephesians 6:1).

• **"Whatever is true, whatever is noble, whatever is right, whatever is pure, whatever is lovely, whatever is admirable—if anything is excellent or praise-worthy—think about such things"** (Philippians 4:8).

• "I can do everything through him who gives me strength" (Philippians 4:13).

• "Faith is being sure of what we hope for and certain of what we do not see" (Hebrews 11:1).

• "Do not merely listen to the word, and so deceive yourselves. Do what it says" (James 1:22).

• "If we confess our sins, he is faithful and just and will forgive us our sins and purify us from all unrighteousness" (I John 1:9).

Point out that the epistles are some of the best sources we have available to us for discovering what is involved in living the Christian life.

5 WHAT AN ENDING!

Say something like: **The last book of the New Testament, the Book of Revelation, is somewhat mysterious. It's written in a symbolic style that's not always easy to decipher. There are several different interpretations of what the book is saying. Fortunately for us, the basic truths of the book can be understood without having to choose a particular interpretation to believe.**

Have volunteers read aloud Revelation 20:1-10.

Then ask: **What comfort can we get from this passage?** (Eventually Satan and all of his evil forces will be defeated forever. We will never have to worry about them again.)

Give group members a few minutes to read through Revelation 21—22.

Afterward, say something like: **We may not understand everything that's described in this passage, but we get the idea that heaven is going to be a pretty incredible place. What stands out to you in this description?** Encourage several volunteers to respond.

Explain that the Book of Revelation may seem intimidating and unclear at first; but like great mystery novels, the more you get into it and discover what's going on, the more enjoyable and interesting it becomes.

As you wrap up the session, emphasize that the New Testament is, in a sense, one long story—the story of what Christ accomplished and how His accomplishments should affect our lives today.

Close the session in prayer.

Four Accounts

Jesus entered the temple area and drove out all who were buying and selling there. He overturned the tables of the money changers and the benches of those selling doves. "It is written," he said to them, "'My house will be called a house of prayer,' but you are making it a 'den of robbers'" (Matthew 21:12, 13).

On reaching Jerusalem, Jesus entered the temple area and began driving out those who were buying and selling there. He overturned the tables of the money changers and the benches of those selling doves, and would not allow anyone to carry merchandise through the temple courts. And as he taught them, he said, "Is it not written: "'My house will be called a house of prayer for all nations'? But you have made it 'a den of robbers'"" (Mark 11:15-17).

THEN HE ENTERED THE TEMPLE AREA AND BEGAN DRIVING OUT THOSE WHO WERE SELLING. "IT IS WRITTEN," HE SAID TO THEM, "'MY HOUSE WILL BE A HOUSE OF PRAYER'; BUT YOU HAVE MADE IT 'A DEN OF ROBBERS'" (LUKE 19:45, 46).

When it was almost time for the Jewish Passover, Jesus went up to Jerusalem. In the temple courts he found men selling cattle, sheep and doves, and others sitting at tables exchanging money. So he made a whip out of cords, and drove all from the temple area, both sheep and cattle; he scattered the coins of the money changers and overturned their tables. To those who sold doves he said, "Get these out of here! How dare you turn my Father's house into a market!" His disciples remembered that it is written: "Zeal for your house will consume me." Then the Jews demanded of him, "What miraculous sign can you show us to prove your authority to do all this?" Jesus answered them, "Destroy this temple, and I will raise it again in three days." The Jews replied, "It has taken forty-six years to build this temple, and you are going to raise it in three days?" But the temple he had spoken of was his body (John 2:13-21).

THE EPISTLE QUIZ

1. In this book, Paul stresses that we are saved not because of any works we do, but because of faith in Christ. (It is the fourth epistle that begins with the word "Paul.") _____

2. In chapter 3, verse 2 of this book, Paul instructs us to "set [our] minds on things above, not on earthly things." (In biblical order, it is the seventh book written by Paul.) _____

3. In the second chapter of this book, Paul clears up some misconceptions about the Lord's return. (This book is the "sequel" to #8.) _____

4. This is the final book Paul wrote before his death. It contains a very famous passage (3:16, 17) that details what Scripture is useful for. (This book is the "sequel" to #20.) _____

5. Paul wrote this letter to a slave owner on behalf of a runaway slave. (It is one of only four epistles with just one chapter.) _____

6. This book contains one of the most famous passages ever written about love (chapter 13). (It is one of only two epistles that contain 16 chapters.) _____

7. This book tells us that "if we ask anything according to [God's] will . . . we know that we have what we asked of him" (5:14, 15). (It is the first of three epistles written by "the disciple whom Jesus loved.") _____

8. This book contains a famous passage (4:13—5:11) describing the coming of Christ. (It is one of the three letters of Paul that have a sequel.) _____

9. This book contains the "Faith Hall of Fame" in chapter 11. (No one knows for sure who wrote this book.) _____

10. This book contains the verse "I can do everything through him who gives me strength" (4:13). (It is one of only three epistles written by Paul that contain four chapters.) _____

11. In the second chapter of this book, the author warns against false teachers. (This book is the "sequel" to #17.) _____

II Peter   II Thessalonians

Philemon

Galatians   Hebrews

I Corinthians

II Timothy

I JOHN

I Thessalonians

Colossians

PHILIPPIANS

12. The emphasis of this book is on God's plan of salvation and righteousness for all people. The book also includes some hard-hitting passages about sin (3:23; 6:23). (Besides I Corinthians, it has more chapters than any other epistle.) _____

13. This book warns against unintentionally supporting false teachers by inviting them into your home. (This book is the "sequel" to #7.) _____

14. This book contains a very famous passage (3:1-12) on controlling our tongues. (Not counting Hebrews, it is one of only two epistles not written by Paul that doesn't have a sequel or isn't a sequel itself.) _____

15. This letter was written to one of Paul's fellow workers, whom Paul had left behind in Crete to organize the church there. (Of all of Paul's epistles, this one has the shortest title.) _____

16. Verse 11 of this book says, "Do not imitate what is evil but what is good." (This is the only epistle addressed to Gaius.) _____

17. In this book, the author instructs us to "rejoice" when we face sufferings for Christ (4:13). (The author of this book was one of Jesus' best friends.) _____

18. Verse 9 of this epistle refers to the dispute over Moses' body between the archangel Michael and Satan. (This epistle has 25 verses in it.) _____

19. In chapters 5 and 6 of this book, Paul provides instructions regarding family relationships and responsibilities. (The name of this epistle is the only one that begins with a vowel.) _____

20. This book contains the famous saying, "The love of money is a root of all kinds of evil" (6:10). (This was the first letter written to Paul's "true son in the faith.") _____

21. In chapter 10 of this book, Paul defends his ministry and his authority against people who claimed he wasn't a true apostle. (This book is the "sequel" to #6.) _____

EPHESIANS

III JOHN

I Peter

JUDE

I Timothy

Titus

II Corinthians

II JOHN

J**AMES**

ROMANS

Session 7

"[The early Christians] devoted themselves to the apostles' teaching and to the fellowship, to the breaking of bread and to prayer. . . . All the believers were together and had everything in common. Selling their possessions and goods, they gave to anyone as he had need. Every day they continued to meet together in the temple courts. They broke bread in their homes and ate together with glad and sincere hearts, praising God and enjoying the favor of all the people" (Acts 2:42-47).

At the risk of sounding flippant—so what? Why should your group members care about the practices of the first-century church? What bearing do the lives of the early Christians have on our lives today? Probably some of your kids will be asking these questions (if not aloud, then to themselves) during this session.

The answer is twofold. First, by examining how the early Christians worked together to fulfill Christ's goals for the church, we get a better understanding of how we can work together today in fulfilling Christ's goals. Second, being reminded of the persecution that early Christians faced for their faith can give us a better appreciation of the importance of Christ's message.

How Did the Church Get Started?

Specific Aims

• To help kids understand how the first-century church got started; to help them understand how the early Christians worked together to fulfill Christ's goals for the church; and to help them compare today's worship/fellowship practices with the practices of the early church.

Scriptural Support

• Matthew 28:18-20
• Acts 2:42-47
• Ephesians 4:11-15
• I Timothy 3:15

Special Preparation

• Bibles
• Copies of Student Sheet 7-A ("Personal Assignments")
• Copies of Student Sheet 7-B ("What Would You Be Willing to Do?")
• Pencils
• Chalkboard and chalk or newsprint and marker
• Adult volunteers (see Step 1)
• Ping-Pong balls
• Wastebasket

1 WHILE THE LEADER'S AWAY . . .

Before the session, you'll need to recruit three or four adults to sit in on the first part of your meeting. Make sure you choose people your kids don't know.

When your kids arrive, explain to them that the adults are a delegation from a church that is trying to start a youth ministry program. These people are in your meeting to observe and take notes on how your group functions.

Ask one of your group members to explain to the delegation how he or she became a part of the group. Ask another to explain how your group plans outreach events. Ask another to explain how your group raises money to fund its activities. As these kids are presenting their explanations, give them a lot of help. Jump in with comments of your own when it looks as though one of them is getting stuck or is running out of things to say.

In the middle of the presentations, you will be called away for "an important phone call." (You'll need to arrange to have someone call you away at the proper time.) As you leave, instruct group members to continue on with the presentation.

Your absence will probably throw your group members for a loop. Chances are they won't know what to say. Your adult volunteers shouldn't help your group members in any way. Kids will probably ask them, "What do you want to know about the group?" If so, your adults should keep their answers vague and general: "We just want to know what goes on in a youth group and what we need to do to begin one." They should also remain passive and unexpressive while group members talk.

After a few minutes, return to the room. Ask: **How did it go while I was gone? Did you explain everything our visitors need to know?** Encourage several group members to respond.

Was it easier to talk to our visitors while I was in the room or was it easier to talk while I was gone? (Probably most of your group members will say that it was easier to talk while you were in the room.) **Why?** (Because they could follow your lead.)

Explain that your visitors really aren't a delegation from another church—they're part of a planned activity. Dismiss them with a round of applause.

Say: **I wanted to give you an idea of what it's like to try to do something you're unsure of without someone to lead you. It's pretty difficult, isn't it?**

Have someone read aloud Matthew 28:18-20.

Say something like: **Many of Jesus' followers had been with Him for almost three years. During that time, they listened to His teaching, watched Him perform miracles, and followed His instructions. And now, in this passage, Jesus says, "I want you to take My message—the things I've taught you—to the entire world. But there's one catch: I won't be here physically to lead you on this mission." After Jesus gave His disciples their mission, He ascended to heaven.**

How do you think Jesus' followers felt after Jesus left? (Scared, unprepared, challenged, discouraged, etc.)

Point out that Jesus' followers had only three choices: reject the mission, pursue it alone, or band together to accomplish it.

2 AGAINST ALL ODDS

Before the session, cut out the cards from a copy of Student Sheet 7-A ("Personal Assignments"). If you have more than nine group members, you'll need to cut apart more than one copy.

Give each group member a card, making sure you evenly distribute cards from the three rows on the sheet. Allow a minute or two for group members to read their assignments and recruit people to help them.

Put a wastebasket at one end of the room and several Ping-Pong balls at the other end. Then say: **You have three minutes to complete your assignments. Go.**

After three minutes, call "time." Discuss the activity, using the following questions.

How difficult was your assignment?

What made it difficult? (The people who were trying to stop me.)

Could you have completed your assignment without the help of other people? Why or why not?

Point out that the early Christians faced extreme opposition as they attempted to complete the assignment Christ gave them.

Say something like: **As if it weren't bad enough for Jesus' followers to have to continue without the physical presence of their leader, they also had to face Jewish leaders and Roman officials who were anxious to stamp out Christianity as quickly as possible. These leaders and officials thought that crucifying Jesus would put an end to Christianity. When it didn't, they wanted to prevent the early Christians from spreading Christ's message. And they were prepared to do whatever it took to stop the Christians—including torturing and killing them.**

Distribute copies of Student Sheet 7-B ("What Would You Be Willing to Do?") and pencils. Give group members a few minutes to complete the sheet. Then ask volunteers to share and explain their responses.

Ask: **If you knew there was a chance that you could be tortured and even killed for talking about Jesus to others, would it affect your actions?** Encourage group members to give the question some thought. Would they *really* be willing to suffer for their faith?

Point out that this was a decision many of the early Christians had to make.

Have volunteers go through the situations on Student Sheet 7-B again and explain how their responses would differ if they had three or four people helping them in each situation.

Ask: **How might the church have been helpful to Christians facing persecution?** (Knowing that they weren't going to be facing persecution alone might have helped Christians make the decision to spread Christ's message. After all, there is strength in numbers.)

Point out that one of the earliest descriptions of the first-century church can be found in Acts 2:42-47. Have someone read aloud the passage.

Ask: **According to this passage, what kinds of day-to-day things went on in the first-century church?** (Listening to the apostles' teaching, Communion, prayer, members spending most of their time together, selling possessions to help the needy, eating together, worship, evangelism, etc.) Write the responses on the board as they are named.

Next to those responses, write the heading "The Lord's Goals for His Church," and numbers 1-3 underneath it.

Say something like: **In Matthew 28:19, we saw one goal the Lord has for His church. What is it?** (To take the message of Christ to the whole world.) Write "To take the message of Christ to the whole world" on the board next to #1.

Have someone read aloud Ephesians 4:11-15.

Ask: **According to this passage, what is another goal the Lord has for His church?** (To become mature in Him.) Write "To become mature in Him" on the board next to #2.

Have someone read aloud I Timothy 3:15.

Ask: **According to this verse, what is another goal the Lord has for His church?** (To be a pillar of truth, dedicated to following Christ's commands.) Write "To be a pillar of truth" on the board next to #3.

3 THE CHURCH: PAST AND PRESENT

Refer to the list on the board of the day-to-day activities of the first-century church. Ask: **How do the activities of our church today compare to the activities of the early church?** (Rather than listening to apostles teach, we listen to the pastor preach. Like the early church, we have Communion, prayer, and worship. Members of our church don't spend most of their time with each other or eat together as often as the members of the early church did. Probably not many of our members sell their possessions to help others in need.)

What has caused some of the differences between the first-century church and the church of today? (Geographically, the members of our church probably aren't as close as the members of the first-century church, so it's not as convenient to get together. Also, because most churches today aren't facing physical persecution, the need for mutual support and encouragement among members may not seem to be as important today as it was in the first century.)

Comparing today's church with the one in the first century, would you say the church has improved in the past two thousand years? Explain your response. Encourage group members to share specific areas in which they feel the church has improved and specific areas in which they feel the church hasn't improved. For instance, someone may say that the church has improved in the area of teaching because pastors today have a wide variety of sources from which to draw their material. Someone else may say that the church hasn't improved in the area of fellowship because members today don't spend enough time together.

You may need to point out that the first-century church was far from perfect, just as today's church is far from perfect. The first-century church had its share of power struggles, false teachers, immorality, greed, divisions, etc.

Note that the goals Christ set for the church could also apply to your group.

Refer to some of the areas identified by your group members in which the church hasn't improved. Ask: **How might some of these areas affect *our group's***

ability to fulfill the Lord's goals? (Lack of fellowship among group members may prevent some of them from becoming spiritually mature; an unwillingness to give up possessions to help the needy may hinder the group's ability to spread the message of Christ; etc.)

Have group members form three teams. Assign each team one of the Lord's goals for the church listed on the board. Instruct each team to brainstorm a list of ways your group could improve its efforts to fulfill that goal.

Ask: **What could our group do to improve its world outreach?**

What could our group do to help members become more spiritually mature?

What could our group do to become more of a "pillar of truth" in the community?

Give the teams several minutes to work. When everyone is finished, ask each team to share its ideas.

Supplement the teams' responses with the following suggestions.

What could our group do to improve its world outreach?

• Invite a missionary to speak to the group about the needs in his or her country.

• Contact a mission organization to find out how the group can contribute to its ministry.

• Organize a fund drive in which members sell some of their possessions and donate the money to the needy.

What could our group do to help members become more spiritually mature?

• Organize small groups to study areas such as personal evangelism, God-honoring money management, and maintaining a personal Bible study.

• Seek out opportunities for members to get involved in various ministries of the church.

What could our group do to become more of a "pillar of truth" in the community?

• Take public stands on issues such as abortion and the environment.

• Help set up homeless shelters and "halfway" houses in your community.

Emphasize to your group members that as they work toward the Lord's goals, they will face opposition—whether it's in the form of lack of personal motivation or a person or group physically trying to stop them. One of the keys to overcoming such opposition is to do what the early Christians did—band together.

Close the session in prayer.

Your assignment is to get five Ping-Pong balls into the wastebasket.

You may need to ask other people in the group to help you with your assignment.

Your assignment is to get five Ping-Pong balls into the wastebasket.

You may need to ask other people in the group to help you with your assignment.

Your assignment is to get five Ping-Pong balls into the wastebasket.

You may need to ask other people in the group to help you with your assignment.

Your assignment is to help the first person who asks for your assistance. You will do whatever he or she asks you to do.

Your assignment is to help the first person who asks for your assistance. You will do whatever he or she asks you to do.

Your assignment is to help the first person who asks for your assistance. You will do whatever he or she asks you to do.

Your assignment is to prevent anyone from picking up the Ping-Pong balls on the floor.

You may need to ask other people in the group to help you with your assignment.

Your assignment is to block anyone trying to carry Ping-Pong balls to the wastebasket.

You may need to ask other people in the group to help you with your assignment.

Your assignment is to prevent anyone from putting Ping-Pong balls in the wastebasket.

You may need to ask other people in the group to help you with your assignment.

WHAT WOULD YOU BE WILLING TO DO?

Use this key to respond to the following situations.
A = I wouldn't be willing to do anything to help.
B = I would be willing to help out a little, but not much.
C = I would be willing to risk injury to myself to help.
D = I would be willing to risk my life to help.

_____ **1.** A car with a flat tire is sitting on the shoulder of a busy interstate. The driver, a teenager who has obviously just recently started driving, stands next to the car helplessly.

_____ **2.** Your worst enemy at school slips while carrying his or her science project to class. The project falls to the floor and breaks into several pieces.

_____ **3.** Your neighbor's cat is stuck in a tree.

_____ **4.** Three football players are picking on a freshman "geek" outside the locker room.

_____ **5.** A young woman is being assaulted by a gang late at night in the park.

_____ **6.** Your best friend's getting pretty heavily involved in the occult.

_____ **7.** An elderly woman has her purse snatched on the street.

_____ **8.** Some kids have never heard about Christ's love and what He's done for them.

Session 8

Kids today are being bombarded with messages stressing the importance of being "politically correct." MTV and other media outlets inform viewers what positions rock stars and other celebrities are taking on political and moral issues. One of the basic tenets of political correctness being stressed by these media is pluralism.

To say that Jesus Christ is the *only* way to God is to violate the pluralistic view that whatever belief is right for you is the right belief. The "politically correct" would say that Hinduism, Islam, Buddhism, and Christianity are all valid belief systems; to suggest that one religion is the exclusive path to eternal happiness is offensive to our hyper-tolerant society.

At the risk of being labeled "intolerant" or "politically incorrect," your kids need to understand that the entire basis for the Christian faith is that Jesus Christ *alone* is the revealed way to eternal life. The fact of His death and resurrection sets apart Christianity from all other religions.

HOW IS CHRISTIANITY DIFFERENT FROM OTHER RELIGIONS?

Specific Aim

• To help group members understand how the death and resurrection of Christ separates Christianity from all other world religions.

Scriptural Support

• Matthew 27:27-54, 57-66; 28:1, 2, 4, 11-15
• Mark 16:1-8
• Luke 24:13-32, 36-49
• John 14:6; 20:11-31
• Acts 9:1-9
• I Corinthians 15:6, 7, 12-19
• Ephesians 2:8, 9
• I John 5:11, 12

Special Preparation

• Bibles
• Copies of Student Sheet 8-A ("Did It Happen?")
• Pencils
• Chalkboard and chalk or newsprint and marker

1 HOMEMADE RELIGION

Have group members form four teams. Instruct each team to come up with its own "religion." The religion may be as elaborate or as zany as team members desire. In creating their religions, the teams must answer three questions:
- **What do you believe?**
- **How do you become a member?**
- **What happens when you die?**

Read the following example to give kids an idea of what you're looking for: **Elvisarians believe that Elvis Presley was abducted by space aliens and declared the King of the Universe. Someday he will return in his flying saucer shaped like a guitar and take all his followers cruising in space forever. In order to be a true believer, you must make an annual pilgrimage to Graceland, wear blue suede shoes and white jumpsuits, and grow sideburns past your earlobes.**

Encourage the teams to be creative, but emphasize that they should not be irreverent in their ideas. Discourage them from using any ideas connected with Christ, His death, or His resurrection.

After all the teams have shared, say: **In the world today there are thousands of different religions. Some of them might seem to us to be as silly as the ones we came up with. Others appear to be very philosophical and seem to make a lot of sense. Most religions share a few things in common. They believe something about God, or a higher power. They have some guidelines regarding how to belong. And they try to provide some answer about what happens to us when this life is over. In this session, we're going to be looking at what sets Christianity apart from the other thousands of religions in the world.**

2 THE LOGICAL PROGRESSION

Draw the following chart on the board.

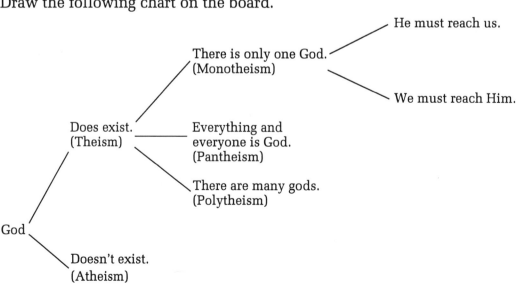

Explain that all religious systems fall basically into these categories. At the most primary level is the decision as to whether or not some type of god exists. Atheists are the only ones who deny entirely the existence of a higher power. Their belief system is based largely on what they don't believe in—namely, God. They believe that life ends at death, period.

All other religious systems believe that there is some power beyond what we can see. These systems can be divided into three categories: monotheists, who believe in one God; pantheists, who believe that God is made up of all things and that everyone and everything is God; and polytheists, who believe in many gods.

Designate one corner of the room "Monotheism"; designate another "Pantheism"; and designate a third corner "Polytheism." As you read descriptions of the following people, group members will move to the corner that they think best describes each person's belief system.

(1) The ancient Greeks who exalted Zeus, Hermes, Apollo, and others as gods. (Polytheism.)

(2) A New Age guru who teaches that all of us are god. (Pantheism.)

(3) A Mormon missionary who tells you that by living right you can become a god just like Jesus became a god. (Polytheism.) [NOTE: The fact that Mormons are polytheistic may be new to your group members since Mormons claim to believe in the one true God. However, their doctrine claims that we all have the potential to become gods ourselves, thus making them polytheistic.]

(4) A Muslim who worships Allah. (Monotheism.)

(5) A Christian who worships the God of the Bible. (Monotheism.)

Point out that among the monotheistic religions, there are two categories: those who believe that we must reach God through our own efforts and those who believe that God has chosen to reach us because we *can't* reach Him.

Have someone read aloud Ephesians 2:8, 9.

Ask: **What "grace" is this passage referring to?** (The undeserved generosity God showed in sending His Son to die for our sins and provide a way for us to have eternal life.)

Other religions believe that if you do enough good works, you can earn your way into eternal life. Why don't Christians believe this? (Christians believe that we could never do enough good works to satisfy a perfect God. Our sin separates us from Him.)

Say something like: **So Christians believe in a loving God who graciously reaches out to people. But that's just one opinion among many. Believing it doesn't make it true. There are many good people who sincerely believe each of the other religions. Like Christianity, these other religions have teachings that help people live moral lives and provide a sense of happiness here and now. But the big question is "What happens when you die?"**

All religions try to answer this question one way or another. The only thing most religions can offer is an unproven opinion. But one belief system rests its case on the historical fact that its leader actually died, remained dead for three days, and then came back to life. If Christ did conquer death, then obviously He is the authority to listen to. If not . . .

Have someone read aloud I Corinthians 15:12-19.

3 Did It Happen?

[NOTE: If your group members aren't familiar with the account of Jesus' crucifixion, it might be helpful to have them quickly read through Matthew 27:27-54. You may also need to explain what was involved in the crucifixion—the beating beforehand by the governor's guards, Jesus' hands and feet being nailed to the cross, etc.]

Ask: **How can we be sure that Christ really rose from the dead after three days?** Encourage several volunteers to offer their opinions. Then suggest that there are at least three lines of evidence that support the truth of the Resurrection: physical proofs, witnesses, and the effects.

Distribute copies of Student Sheet 8-A ("Did It Happen?") and pencils. Direct group members' attention to the first section of the sheet, "The Theories."

Say something like: **Many theories have been given about the Resurrection that attempt to explain it away. Yet most of these theories can be disproved by one rock—the one placed over the entrance of the tomb in which Jesus was buried.**

Have someone read aloud Matthew 27:57—28:2. Point out that the stone that was rolled in front of the tomb probably weighed between three thousand and four thousand pounds.

Say: **Take a look at the three theories on your sheet that attempt to explain Jesus' resurrection. Think about the facts that we've just talked about. Then put an "X" next to the theories that you think are discredited by the facts.**

Give group members several minutes to work. Then have volunteers share and explain their responses.

Use the following information to supplement their answers.

(1) The disciples sneaked past the guards and stole the body. Point out that Roman guards were armed and well trained. If they failed at their post, they would be executed. There is no chance that eleven guys could just sneak past them and roll away a two-ton boulder without being noticed. Furthermore, the penalty for breaking a Roman seal, like the one on Jesus' tomb, was immediate death. It is doubtful that a group of disillusioned disciples would have risked so much for a scam.

(2) Jesus only passed out on the cross—He didn't die. When He awoke later in the tomb, He rolled away the stone and escaped. Point out that this theory, commonly known as the "swoon theory," is absurd from a physical standpoint. How could a man suffering from severe blood loss, with open wounds and extreme nerve and muscle damage in His hands, feet, and side, who has been left in a coma without medical attention for three days, single-handedly move a two-ton boulder and run away (and then inspire His followers to live and die for Him)?

(3) The power of God, through an angel, moved the stone to show everyone that Christ had risen. Suggest that this is the only logical answer. Point out that Jesus didn't *need* the stone moved. Luke 24:36-49 tells us that Jesus startled His disciples by suddenly appearing to them inside a locked room. He could have gotten out of the tomb without moving the stone. The stone was moved so everyone else could see inside the tomb and know that He had risen.

Point out to your group members that the religious leaders of the day wanted to stop the rumors that Jesus had risen.

Ask: **What one piece of evidence could the Pharisees have produced to put a stop to the rumors once and for all?** (Christ's body.) Suggest that the fact that they couldn't locate Christ's body seems to strengthen the case for the Resurrection.

Direct group members' attention to the second section of the sheet, "The Witnesses."

Ask: **If you were trying to prove a point in a court of law, what's the most important thing you would need to help your case?** (Eyewitnesses.)

Say something like: **There were several eyewitnesses to Jesus' resurrection. But before we use their testimony to prove our case, we need to determine whether those witnesses were reliable or not. In order for witnesses to be reliable, they must have three qualities: (1) the witnesses must have had personal involvement in the situation; (2) the witnesses must have good reputations; and (3) there must be enough witnesses to verify the facts.**

Have your group members form pairs. Instruct the pairs to complete the chart on Student Sheet 8-A by looking up the passages and answering the questions. When everyone is finished, have volunteers call out their responses.

Use the following information to supplement the pairs' answers.

Verses	Who were they?	Were they involved?	Did they have good character?	How many were there?
Mark 16:1-8	Women	Yes	Yes	3
John 20:11-18	Mary	Yes	Yes	1
Luke 24:13-32	Disciples	Yes	Yes	2
John 20:19-25	Disciples	Yes	Yes	10
John 20:26-31	Thomas/ Disciples	Yes	Yes	1+10
I Corinthians 15:6	Followers	Yes	Yes	500
I Corinthians 15:7	James/Paul/ Apostles	Yes	Yes	1+1+11
Matthew 28:4, 11-15	Guards	Yes	No	???
Acts 9:1-9	Saul (Paul)	Yes	Yes	1

Ask: **If you were on a jury for a murder trial and the defendant brought in over five hundred witnesses who said they were with him at the time the murder was committed, would it be enough to convince you to find the defendant not guilty?**

There were over five hundred witnesses to Jesus' resurrection. Is that enough to convince you that Jesus really rose from the dead? Encourage several group members to respond.

Direct group members' attention to the third section on the sheet, "The Effects."

Say something like: **One other theory used to explain away Christ's resurrection is that it was just a hoax carried off by His disciples. This theory claims that Jesus never rose from the dead, but that His disciples claimed He did. They wrote about His supposed resurrection in the books that later became our New Testament. Therefore, Christianity is based on a myth.**

However, tradition and history tell us that probably all but one of Jesus' eleven disciples (Judas had committed suicide) **were killed because of their Christian beliefs. Think about that for a minute. Then write down what you believe is wrong with the theory.**

Give group members a few minutes to work. Then ask volunteers to share their responses. If no one mentions it, suggest that people will die for what they believe to be *true,* but not what they know is a lie. To escape death, all the disciples would have had to do was admit that they made up the story of Jesus' resurrection. But they weren't willing to do that because they actually *believed* that Jesus had risen.

4 Making It Personal

Have someone read aloud John 14:6.

Say: **Other religions believe that there are other ways to God than through Jesus. Do you think it's narrow-minded of Christians to believe that Jesus is the *only* way?** If no one mentions it, emphasize that Jesus declared Himself to be the only way. In Step 3, we demonstrated His authority over things eternal—so if *He* says He's the only way, we should take His word for it.

As you wrap up the session, read aloud I John 5:11, 12. Give group members who aren't Christians an opportunity to accept the gift of life through Jesus Christ. Then close the session in prayer.

Did It Happen?

The Theories

- ☐ The disciples sneaked past the guards and stole the body.
- ☐ Jesus only passed out on the cross—He didn't die. When He awoke later in the tomb, He rolled away the stone and escaped.
- ☐ The power of God, through an angel, moved the stone to show everyone that Christ had risen.

The Witnesses

Verses	Who were they?	Were they involved?	Did they have good character?	How many were there?
Mark 16:1-8				
John 20:11-18				
Luke 24:13-32				
John 20:19-25				
John 20:26-31				
I Corinthians 15:6				
I Corinthians 15:7				
Matthew 28:4, 11-15				
Acts 9:1-9				

The Effects

What's wrong with the following theory?

Christ's resurrection was just a hoax planned by His disciples. Jesus never rose from the dead, but (for whatever reasons) His disciples claimed He did. They wrote about His supposed resurrection in the books that later became our New Testament. Therefore, Christianity is based on a myth.

Session 9

How many non-Christians do you have in your group? Have you ever asked them why they haven't accepted Christ? If asked, some of them might cite the "hassle" involved. They've mistaken the *manifestations* of the Christian life—church attendance, Bible study, service to others—with the process of becoming a Christian. Others may feel that they're not "good enough" to become a Christian or that they're not really the "Christian type."

Help your group members see that not only is Christ available to everyone (regardless of background), but also the process of becoming a Christian is relatively simple.

Admit that you're a sinner; ask God for forgiveness; believe in Christ's death and resurrection; turn from your sin; and invite Jesus into your life. That's what it takes to become a Christian. Presented in such simple, concrete terms, salvation may be more appealing (and less intimidating) to your non-Christian group members.

This session is designed to introduce salvation to your non-Christian group members, and to reassure those who have accepted Christ, but who may be doubting the validity of that experience.

HOW DO I BECOME A CHRISTIAN?

Specific Aims

• To help kids understand that sin separated us from God—but that God sent His Son to take the punishment for our sins and to restore our relationship with Him; and to help them understand exactly what they have to do to accept Christ as their Savior.

Scriptural Support

• Isaiah 53:6a; 59:2
• John 1:12; 3:16; 10:10; 14:6
• Romans 3:23; 6:23a
• II Corinthians 5:21
• Galatians 2:20
• Ephesians 2:8
• I Timothy 2:5
• I Peter 2:24
• Revelation 3:20

Special Preparation

• Bibles
• Copies of Student Sheet 9-A ("Investigative Reporting")
• Copies of Student Sheet 9-B ("The Eternal Maze")
• Copies of Student Sheet 9-C ("More Investigative Reporting")
• Pencils
• Chalkboard and chalk or newsprint and marker
• Masking tape
• Several Frisbees

1 ACROSS THE GREAT DIVIDE

Before the session, mark off a section of the room with strips of masking tape. The strips should run from wall to wall and should be several feet apart.

As group members arrive, have them form pairs. Instruct the members of each pair to stand on opposite sides of the room, separated by the marked-off area.

Say something like: **The object of this game is for those of you on the right side of the room to get across the marked-off area—without touching the ground—and "rescue" your partners. Of course, none of you can jump that far, so I've got something to help you get across.** Distribute a large Frisbee to each person on the right side of the room. **To get to your partner, you must stand on top of your Frisbee and, using just your body movement, "scoot" across the marked-off area. Then, when you get to the other side, you must figure out a way to get your partner back across with you.** Emphasize that neither of the partners may touch the ground in the marked-off area. If they do, they must start over again.

Give group members about five minutes to complete the activity. Probably very few, if any, of the pairs will be able to finish in that time. When the activity is over, briefly discuss what was difficult about it. Ask group members to suggest easier ways to cross the marked-off area.

Then say something like: **In this session, we're going to be talking about a gap much larger than the one in this activity. In fact, we're going to be talking about the largest chasm imaginable.**

2 UNDER INVESTIGATION

Distribute copies of Student Sheet 9-A ("Investigative Reporting") and pencils. Have group members reassemble into the pairs they formed earlier. Explain that each pair is an investigative reporting team, looking for leads concerning the chasm you just mentioned.

Say something like: **All of your leads for the story come from one source: the Bible. Look up each lead and write down some notes about what it says. Then, after you've investigated all the leads, put your facts together and come up with a possible headline for the story.** Emphasize that the headlines should be short, attention-getting, and to the point.

Give the pairs several minutes to work. When everyone is finished, ask volunteers to share their responses.

Use the following suggestions to supplement the pairs' ideas.

Lead #1—Romans 3:23—Everyone has sinned against God.

Lead #2—Isaiah 59:2—Our sin has separated us from God.

Lead #3—Isaiah 53:6a—Because of our sin, we choose to follow our own way, rather than following God's way.

Lead #4—Romans 6:23a—The penalty for our sin is death. [NOTE: You might want to point out that the "death" referred to here is spiritual death (eternal separation from God), not physical death.]

Possible headlines might include the following: "Everyone Guilty—Death Penalty Set," "Sin Destroys God-Person Relationship," "Sin Blamed for Separation from God," etc.

Ask: **If these four verses were the only part of Scripture you knew, how would they make you feel?** (Scared, hopeless—like there was nothing that could be done about my sin, etc.)

Why does our sin separate us from God? (Because God is perfect and holy, He can never find sin acceptable.)

3 ONLY ONE WAY

Say something like: **People have suggested many different ways for us to restore our relationship with God after we've sinned. Let's look at three of those suggestions now.**

Distribute copies of Student Sheet 9-B ("The Eternal Maze"). Instruct group members to complete the maze to discover which of the methods can restore our relationship with God.

After a couple of minutes, ask volunteers to share their conclusions. Point out that the maze can't be completed because all three paths lead to dead ends. None of these three methods can restore our relationship with God.

Briefly discuss why each method can't restore our relationship with God.

Living a Moral Life—One sin is enough to separate us from God. None of us can live a moral enough life to please God.

Helping the Poor and Needy—We cannot earn reconciliation with God through works—no matter how much we help the poor and needy.

Going to Church—Again, we cannot restore our relationship with God through works. We can't expect to be reconciled with Him because we have a perfect church attendance record.

[NOTE: You may want to point out that these acts often are *results* of (not catalysts for) a restored relationship with God. When people find the way to restore their relationship with God, their lives are changed. Part of this change is the desire to live a moral life, help the needy, and go to church.]

Have group members reassemble into their pairs. Distribute copies of Student Sheet 9-C ("More Investigative Reporting"). Explain that the investigative teams will be tracking leads for a new story.

Say something like: **As with your first story, all of your leads for this story come from the Bible. Look up each lead and write down some notes about what it says. Then, after you've investigated all the leads, put your facts together and come up with a possible headline for the story.**

Give the pairs several minutes to work. When everyone is finished, ask volunteers to share their responses.

Use the following suggestions to supplement the pairs' ideas.

Lead #1—II Corinthians 5:21; I Peter 2:24—Jesus, who was sinless, took our sins upon Himself.

Lead #2—Galatians 2:20; I Timothy 2:5—Christ lives in those for whom He died. Jesus died to bridge the gap between God and us.

Lead #3—John 1:12; 14:6—We can enter God's family, but we must do it through Christ. He's the only way.

Lead #4—Ephesians 2:8—Through Jesus, God offers us the gift of eternal life.

Lead #5—John 3:16; 10:10; Revelation 3:20—Through Jesus, God offers us an alternative to darkness. God loved us enough to send His Son. We must open the door to Him.

Possible headlines might include the following: "God Offers Opportunity for Reconciliation," "Christ's Sacrifice Makes Eternal Life Possible," "Gap Bridged between God and People," etc.

Ask: **How do you feel, knowing that Christ has provided a way for us to restore our relationships with God?** (Grateful, relieved, curious about what I have to do exactly to take advantage of Christ's offer.)

4 STEP-BY-STEP

Say something like: **God has offered us a way to restore our relationship with Him and avoid being separated from Him forever. But the choice is ours as to whether or not we want to accept His offer. If we accept, we start a relationship with Him that will last forever. If we don't accept—or if we ignore His offer—we face eternal separation from Him.**

At this point in the session, you'll want to present a clear, step-by-step explanation of exactly what a person must do to become a Christian. Use the following points to supplement your explanation. (Write each major point on the board as you explain it.)

1. We must admit our need for Christ.

The Bible is clear on the point that all of us have sinned. Any selfish thought, unkind word, or rebellious action is a violation of God's standards—and is enough to separate us from Him. We must recognize that there is nothing we can do by ourselves to bridge the gap that sin creates between people and God. The Lord's standards are just too high.

2. We must believe that Jesus died on the cross for us and then rose from the dead.

Jesus is the only answer to our problem. Christ made our rescue possible, meeting God's requirements, when He died on the cross. According to the Bible, He took the punishment for our sins. The gap that stood between us and God was bridged by the cross. The death of Christ was necessary for God to put away our sins forever. Then after He died on the cross, to show His power over sin and death, Jesus Christ rose from the grave. He now sits at the right hand of His heavenly Father!

3. We must turn away from our sins.

It's not enough to just admit our sins to God. It's not even enough to feel sorry for what we've done. God calls us to turn our backs on the things in our lives that we know are wrong and to allow Christ to clean us up inside. This may not happen immediately. Many people gradually surrender areas of their lives to Christ as the Holy Spirit works in their hearts to convict them of sin. The point is that when a person becomes a Christian, he or she must be willing to have a new master in charge of his or her life.

4. We must invite Jesus to come into our lives.

Jesus won't "force" Himself on us. He waits to be invited. He wants to start a new relationship with us. But God has given us the ability to make choices. Some people choose not to become Christians.

Ask: **What reasons might people give for not accepting Christ into their lives?** (They want to run their own lives. They're afraid they won't have "fun" anymore. They're afraid of how others may react.) Point out that the benefits of becoming a Christian far outweigh any "disadvantages" we might think of.

5 PERSONAL REFLECTION

Ask group members to bow their heads and silently examine where they stand with Christ. Invite those who wish to accept Christ or reaffirm a past decision for Christ to pray silently with you. Instead of leading them in a prayer, give them suggestions as to what to pray about (using the principles in Step 4) and let them silently formulate the prayer in their own words. First, have them acknowledge their sinfulness before God and admit their need for a Savior. Then ask them to express to the Lord their belief in the death and resurrection of Christ—and the fact that He gave His life for them. Instruct them to tell God they want to turn away from their sins and follow Christ. Have them invite Jesus into their lives, placing their complete trust in Him for salvation.

To close, have all group members stand in a circle and hold hands. Give group members an opportunity to pray for one another as they begin their new lives with Christ.

As group members leave, invite those who want to talk more about becoming a Christian to meet with you after the session.

INVESTIGATIVE REPORTING

Look up each of the following leads and write down some notes about what it says. Then, after you've investigated all the leads, put your facts together and come up with a possible headline for the story.

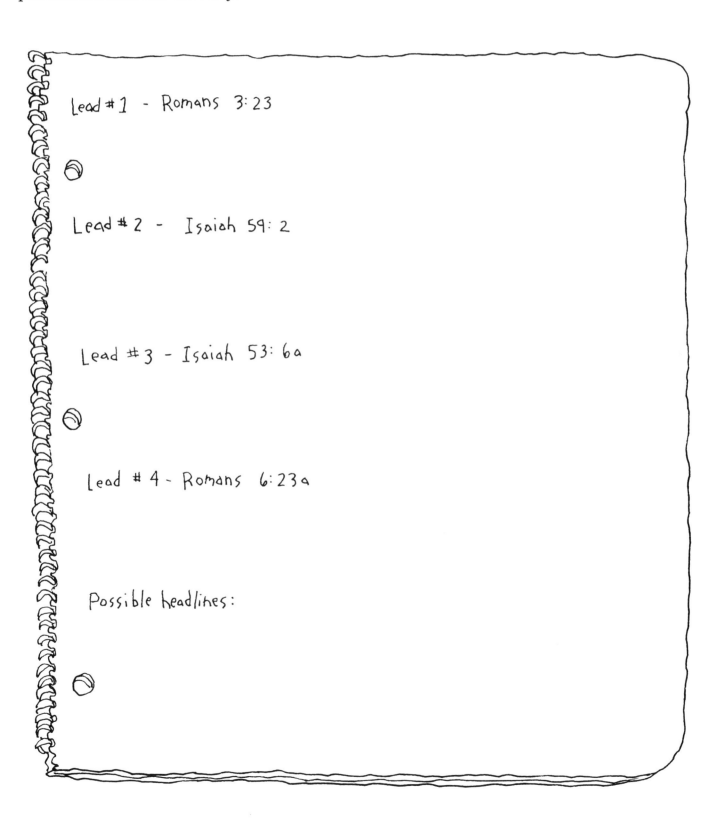

Lead #1 - Romans 3:23

Lead #2 - Isaiah 59:2

Lead #3 - Isaiah 53:6a

Lead #4 - Romans 6:23a

Possible headlines:

THE ETERNAL MAZE

Complete the maze to discover which of the three methods leads to a restored relationship with God.

LIVING A MORAL LIFE

Helping the Poor and Needy

Going to Church

GOD

More Investigative Reporting

Look up each of the following leads and write down some notes about what it says. Then, after you've investigated all the leads, put your facts together and come up with a possible headline for the story.

Lead #1 - II Corinthians 5:21; I Peter 2:24

Lead #2 - Galatians 2:20; I Timothy 2:5

Lead #3 - John 1:12; 14:6

Lead #4 - Ephesians 2:8

Lead #5 - John 3:16; 10:10; Revelation 3:20

Possible headlines:

Session 10

Making Jesus "Lord of your life" is something all *adults* should do. For kids, it's enough just to be a Christian, to ask Jesus into your heart. Living for Him and turning over areas of your life to His control are grown-up responsibilities. After all, if you turned over *all* the areas of your life to Jesus, you'd never have any fun. And since adults don't really have much fun anyhow, it's not that bad for them.

You might be surprised at how many of your group members hold similar opinions about making Jesus Lord of their lives.

The mandate from Scripture is clear and all-inclusive: Since Jesus Christ is the eternal Creator and Ruler of all, He must have first place in our hearts. He calls us to examine each and every facet of our lives, submitting those areas that are not under His rule and praising Him for the areas that are.

WHAT DOES IT MEAN TO LET JESUS BE SAVIOR *AND* LORD OF MY LIFE?

Specific Aims

• To help kids understand the need not only to accept Christ as Savior, but also to give Him complete lordship over every area of their lives; to explain what "giving Him lordship" entails; and to help kids think of areas in their lives that they need to turn over to Jesus' lordship.

Scriptural Support

• Romans 6:13; 12:1, 2
• I Corinthians 6:19, 20
• Philippians 2:5-11
• Colossians 1:16
• James 4:7a
• I John 2:3, 4

Special Preparation

• Bibles
• Copies of Student Sheet 10-A ("Excuses, Excuses")
• Copies of Student Sheet 10-B ("Who's the Boss?")
• Pencils
• Desserts prepared according to the instructions in Step 1
• Blindfold
• Slips of paper prepared according to the instructions in Step 3

1 THE MISSING INGREDIENT

Before the session, you'll need to prepare three desserts. In doing so, however, you should leave out a key ingredient of each dessert. For instance, if you were making oatmeal cookies, you might leave out the oatmeal or the sugar. You might also make a chocolate cake without any chocolate or a lemon pie without any lemon flavoring. The object is to prepare three foods that will not taste like they should, because you've failed to include an important ingredient.

To open the session, ask for a volunteer to participate in a taste test. Send the volunteer out of the room while you prepare for the taste test. Place the three desserts on a table, explaining to the rest of the group that all the volunteer has to do is taste each item and guess what it is. Blindfold the volunteer and bring him or her back into the room.

Have the volunteer sample the first item and tell the group what it is. If the item is a cookie, the volunteer must identify what *kind* of cookie it is. The volunteer will probably have difficulty identifying what kind of cookie it is. If so, don't allow him or her a lot of time to guess. Instead, have him or her move on to the second item. Repeat the process for all three items.

Remove the volunteer's blindfold and pretend to be bewildered at his or her inability to identify the items. Distribute the remaining cookies, pieces of cake, and/or slices of pie to the rest of the group members. Wait for their reactions.

Then say something like: **I have a confession to make. In preparing these foods, I deliberately left out some important ingredients. When you leave sugar out of a cookie recipe, it makes a big difference in the taste. If you leave the lemon flavoring out of a lemon pie, you've left out what makes it distinctive. In the same way, some people try to leave an important ingredient out of the Christian life. We'll find out what it is in a moment.**

2 WHAT IS LORDSHIP?

Play an "agree or disagree" game with the group. Read each of the following statements one at a time. After each statement, have all the group members who agree with the statement stand on one side of the room and all who disagree stand on the other side of the room. (No one may abstain from responding.) After each statement is read, ask volunteers from each side to explain why they responded as they did.

Here are the statements to be used:
- **People are capable of wisely running their own lives.**
- **No one knows better than you what is best for your life.**
- **Blind obedience gets you nowhere.**
- **Jesus is interested in helping us with the *major* decisions of our lives, not the minor details.**
- **Jesus has the right to control *every* area of our lives.**

After reading this last statement, encourage most of your group members to explain their responses.

To those who agreed with the statement, ask: **Why does Jesus have the right to control every area of your life? What has He done to "deserve" that privilege?**

To those who disagreed with the statement, ask: **Which areas of your life do you feel don't necessarily have to be controlled by Jesus? Why?**

To the entire group, ask: **How many of you have heard Jesus called "Lord"?** (Probably most of your group members have.)

Explain that crowning Jesus "Lord of your life" involves allowing Him to control *every* part of your life. Suggest that a person's Christian life isn't complete until he or she crowns Jesus "Lord." Until he or she does that, an "ingredient" is missing in his or her relationship with Christ.

3 WHO'S IN CHARGE HERE?

Before the session, you will need to write each of the following passages on a slip of paper.

    #1—I Corinthians 6:20
    #2—Colossians 1:16
    #3—I Corinthians 6:19
    #4—I John 2:3
    #5—James 4:7a
    #6—Philippians 2:5-7
    #7—Romans 12:1
    #8—Romans 12:2
    #9—Romans 6:13
#10—Philippians 2:10

Say something like: **Let's take a look at what the Bible says about making Jesus Savior *and* Lord of your life. Then we'll create a list of the "Top Ten Reasons to Make Jesus Lord of Your Life."**

Have group members form pairs. Depending on the size of your group, distribute one or more slips of paper to each pair. Instruct each pair to look up its assigned passage and come up with a reason (based on the passage) for making Jesus Lord of your life.

Give the pairs a few minutes to work. When everyone is finished, ask each pair to share its reason. List the reasons on the board as they are named.

Use the following suggestions to supplement the pairs' reasons. (Counting backward from ten to one "heightens the drama" in presenting the top ten list.)

#10—Philippians 2:10—One day every knee will bow to Christ—willingly or unwillingly. By making Him Lord now, we are, in effect, "joining the winning team."

#9—Romans 6:13—Christ wants to use us as tools for accomplishing His goals. By making Jesus Lord, we are allowing ourselves to become part of God's plan.

#8—Romans 12:2—We will discover the will of God, what He wants for our lives.

#7—Romans 12:1—Surrendering our lives to Christ is a way to worship Him.

#6—Philippians 2:5-7—We should have a servant's attitude just as Christ did. Our service should be to Him.

#5—James 4:7a—We are commanded to submit to God.

#4—I John 2:3—Submission proves our relationship with Christ.

#3—I Corinthians 6:19—A Christian's body is the temple of the Holy Spirit. We have no real claim of control or ownership of it.

#2—Colossians 1:16—We were created "for Him"—that is, to serve the Lord.

#1—I Corinthians 6:20—We were bought at a price. In effect, we "owe" it to Christ to make Him Lord.

Explain that these reasons really can't be put in order of importance. They are all vital to understanding why Christ has the authority to be Lord of our lives.

Ask: **How is it an "act of worship" (Romans 12:1) to submit areas of our lives to Christ?** (As we give each area of our lives to Jesus, we are acknowledging His right to be our master.)

What do you think I Corinthians 6:20 means when it says we were "bought at a price"? (Jesus gave His life on the cross for us.) **What difference should this make in our response to Him?** (We should let Him rule our lives out of gratitude for sacrificing Himself for us.)

Have group members reassemble into the pairs they formed earlier. Instruct each pair to brainstorm ways in which the following people's behavior, attitudes, and lifestyles would be different if they gave Jesus control of their lives: a popular rock star, a supermarket tabloid writer, a teenager having problems with his or her parents, and a high-school senior confused about what to do after graduation.

Give the pairs about four minutes to work. Then have each pair share its responses.

Use the following suggestions to supplement the pairs' ideas.

A popular rock star—This person's behavior might change to reflect more Christlike values. If his or her music had glorified premarital sex, drugs, and getting drunk, he or she might begin to glorify God.

A supermarket tabloid writer—He or she may stop writing gossip and made-up "news." Instead, he or she might commit to reporting only the truth.

A teenager having problems with his or her parents—That relationship would probably improve because he or she would be demonstrating Christlike relationship skills.

A high-school senior confused about what to do after graduation—This person might experience less stress about the future because he or she is trusting in Christ's guidance.

Say something like: **The bottom line is that Jesus deserves to be in control of all areas of our lives. We are each faced with the question "Am I going to run my life, or will I let Jesus—who loved me enough to die for me—be the master?" First John 2:4 tells us that if we claim to know Jesus, but don't allow Him rightful ownership of our lives, we are liars.**

4 WHAT'S THE HOLDUP?

Say something like: **We've looked at ten reasons that we *should* make Jesus Lord of our lives. Now let's take a look at some reasons that people *don't* give Him control over some areas of their lives.**

Distribute copies of Student Sheet 10-A ("Excuses, Excuses"). Have a volunteer read aloud each situation. Then, as a group, discuss possible explanations for why the person in each situation failed to surrender a particular area of his or her life to Christ.

Use the following information to supplement discussion of the sheet.

Situation #1—By refusing to tell the teacher what he saw, Stan was failing to let Jesus be Lord of his life at school. He was reluctant to do what was right, probably because he was afraid—afraid not only of what Jeff might do to him but also of what his classmates might think of him. Stan was unwilling to do what was right and leave the consequences in the Lord's hands.

Situation #2—Pam failed to surrender her study habits to the Lord. She may have been afraid that if she showed more responsibility and took her teachers seriously, she wouldn't have as much time to spend with her friends.

Situation #3—David failed to surrender his relationship with his parents to the Lord. Probably one of the primary reasons was David's pride and sense of independence. Obeying his father's instruction to mow the lawn before dinner might have seemed like a loss of freedom and individual choice for David. Backing down from an argument with his father might have seemed like a blow to David's pride.

Say something like: **It's not always easy to let Christ rule over our lives, but it's always worth the effort! Over and over again, the Bible gives us examples of how God rewards faithfulness. It's quite a deal when you think about it. The Lord will bless you for giving Him what's rightfully His to begin with. Making Jesus Lord of your entire life isn't something that will happen overnight. As you discover areas of your life that are in your grasp—and not His—you can turn them over to Him one at a time.**

5 TAKING INVENTORY

Distribute copies of Student Sheet 10-B ("Who's the Boss?") and pencils. Give group members a few minutes to complete the sheet. Emphasize that responses will remain private—no one will be asked to share what he or she wrote.

When everyone is finished, have group members select one area that they marked "I Control." Instruct them to pray silently, asking the Lord to take control over the area. After a few minutes, lead the group in prayer. Ask God to help each group member begin to surrender to the lordship of Christ.

In closing, have group members stand and read aloud in unison Philippians 2:5-11. Remind them that Jesus set the example for us by submitting to His heavenly Father—and He will help us follow that example.

SITUATION #1

Jeff is one of the biggest members of the football team. His size and strength often work in his favor when it comes to getting away with things at school.

In the middle of geometry class, the teacher was called to the office, leaving the class unattended. She left a copy of an upcoming test facedown on her desk. As soon as she left, Jeff sneaked up to her desk, picked up the test, took it back to his desk, and copied some of the questions. When he heard the teacher returning, Jeff returned the test to her desk—faceup.

The teacher knew someone had looked at the test. After failing to get anyone to confess, she took each student—one at a time—into the hallway and questioned him or her. No one admitted to having seen anyone take the test. Stan, who is a Christian, was the last to be questioned. He, too, denied having seen anyone take the test.

SITUATION #2

Pam is failing English class. Her problem is her inability to focus on her homework. After all, she reasons, how can anybody be expected to study when there are so many good TV shows to watch, so much shopping to do, and so many phone calls to make? For Pam, any excuse is a good excuse not to study.

The English teacher had been lenient with Pam, telling her that if she did well on the final exam, she could still pass the course (barely). Pam promised herself she would study. The night before the exam, Pam's best friend (who is in a different English class) asked Pam to go to the opening of a long-awaited movie. Against her better judgment, Pam went. Her final exam score was 52.

SITUATION #3

David never really gets along with his mother and father very well. After all, there are other things to do in life besides catering to his parents' every whim. The biggest, loudest arguments between David and his parents usually start because of David's failure to mow the lawn when asked. This time was no different.

David was asked by his father to mow the lawn before dinner. At 5:45, fifteen minutes before dinner, David still hadn't mowed the lawn. In fact, he was at a friend's house, lifting weights. When David walked in at 6:00, David's father was at the kitchen door. A shouting match began. The argument ended with David going to his room and locking the door while his dad mowed the lawn.

WHO'S THE BOSS?

Think about each of the following areas of your life. If you tend to make decisions in that area on your own, put an "X" in the first column. If you've turned that area over to Christ's control, put an "X" in the second column. If you're unsure who controls that area, put an "X" in the third column.

	I CONTROL	CHRIST CONTROLS	UNSURE
Choices of who to date and where to go			
Relationship with parents			
Non-romantic relationships with the opposite sex			
Who to listen to for advice			
Choices of how to spend my time			
What classes to take			
Music choices			
Amount of time I spend praying and reading the Bible on my own			
Using alcohol/drugs			
Plans for my future			
What I do when I'm angry			
Fears			
The way I see myself			
Clothes			
Language			
How I react to stress			
Sharing my faith			
Choosing friends			
What I think about			

Session 11

Church can and should be a nurturing, loving place to grow in Christ. Unfortunately, for many kids it has become a place of confusion and boredom. One key to helping kids understand the importance of church is to get them to stop thinking in terms of *going* to church and instead get them to think about *being* the church. After all, as part of Christ's body, Christian teenagers are an important part of the church.

There may be no question in your mind about the importance of collective worship, study, fellowship, and ministry. After all, we are commanded by Scripture to gather together as a family of faith, to be the body of Christ. Can you communicate that to your young people? This session should help.

WHY IS CHURCH IMPORTANT?

Specific Aims

• To help kids understand that as the body of Christ, we are the church; to help kids recognize that God is with us as we struggle to know ourselves, each other, and Him; and to encourage kids to become part of the solution in making church activities more meaningful.

Scriptural Support

• John 17
• Romans 12:4, 5
• I Corinthians 12:4-27

Special Preparation

• Bibles
• Copies of Student Sheet 11-A ("The Inventor's Plans")
• Copies of Student Sheet 11-B ("Body Talk")
• Pencils
• Paper
• Building blocks
• Volleyball
• Team prize (optional)

1 PATENT OFFICE

Announce that you're turning your meeting place into a patent office—a place where inventors bring their new inventions. Form teams, and ask each team to come up with an invention that does one of the following:
- Warns you an hour in advance that a teacher is going to give you a pop quiz.
- Washes your hair while you listen to the radio.
- Convinces your parents to let you stay out two hours later than usual.
- Lets a person of the opposite sex know you're interested in him or her, but does so without embarrassing anyone.
- Clips your toenails while you have your shoes on.
- Lets you hit the basket from mid-court every time you try.

Give each team a couple of sheets of paper and a pencil, so that "blueprints" can be drawn. Tell the group that each invention must be explained as fully as possible.

After letting kids work on this for about five minutes, have teams present their inventions to each other. If you like, award a prize for the most original or best-explained invention.

Then ask: **What was the hardest thing about coming up with your invention? What was easiest?**

Let's look at another invention. How hard would it be to come up with an invention that would do the following jobs? After I read each job, if you think it would be impossible, stand up. If you think it would be no problem, sit down. If your answer is somewhere in between, stand up halfway.

Here are the jobs your invention would have to do:
- **Show people how to live forever.**
- **Feed the hungry all over the world.**
- **Communicate with invisible beings.**
- **Enable people to get along in spite of their differences.**

After kids react, explain that you're talking about something that's already been invented—the church.

2 BACK TO THE DRAWING BOARD

Ask: **Who started our church?** If you know a little history about the beginning of your congregation, you may want to share it. But point out that the real founder of the church is Jesus Christ.

Why do you think Jesus invented the church?

After hearing some opinions, pass out copies of Student Sheet 11-A ("The Inventor's Plans"). Give kids a few minutes to read some of Jesus' goals for the church (from John 17), and to decide which parts of a church program might help accomplish those goals. Encourage kids to write in other parts of your church or youth program that might help achieve each goal.

Then ask: **On a scale of 1 to 10 (with 10 being perfect), how well do you think our church meets each of the goals on this sheet? Why?**

On the same scale, how well do you think our youth group does in each area? Why?

Are there some parts of our church program that don't seem to meet any important goals? If so, why do you think our church does these things?

As needed, point out that some church activities meet goals that are important not to us, but to someone else. For instance, elderly homebound church members might appreciate a tape ministry, even if teenagers don't seem to benefit from it. And teenagers can benefit from helping out with a part of the church program (like a tape ministry, children's church, etc.) that serves another age group.

If you were going to invent a church from scratch, how would it be different from ours? How would it be similar? Why?

How do you think the world might be different if there were no church?

3 SUBVERSIVE ACTIONS   *Game w/ Balls*

Before the session, meet privately with two volunteers from your group. Explain that in this activity, you will be dividing the group into two teams and giving each team an assignment to complete. Each of the volunteers will be on one of the teams. Instruct each of the volunteers to do whatever he or she can to hinder his or her team's progress—without being obvious about it. For instance, if a team's assignment is to carry building blocks to a certain part of the room and build a tower with them, the person might "inadvertently" get in his or her teammates' way, "accidentally" knock over the tower, or complain about their efforts.

At this point in the session, divide the group into teams (making certain you put one of your volunteers on each team).

Assign the teams the following tasks.

Team #1—Give the team a pile of building blocks. Say: **Your assignment is to carry these blocks to the other side of the room—one at a time—and build a tower with them. Each person will carry one block, stack it, and then come back for another. You will have two minutes to use all of the blocks in the pile.** (You may need to adjust the time limit, based on how many blocks you use.)

Team #2—Give the team a volleyball. Say: **Your assignment is to hit this ball twenty-five times without allowing it to touch the ground or any other object in the room. If it hits the ground or an object in the room, you must start over. Everyone in the group must hit the ball at least twice. You will have two minutes to do this.**

During the activity, pay attention to how each team responds to the person who is trying to undermine its efforts. If your volunteers are successful in their efforts, neither team should complete its assignment in the allotted time.

Afterward, explain the volunteers' assignment to the rest of the group members. Then ask: **How difficult was it for your team to complete its task when one of your teammates was trying to mess you up?** (Very difficult.)

Say something like: **There's another "team" whose task is often made more difficult by its members. The team I'm talking about is the church.**

How do people make it tough for the church to accomplish the goals the Lord has set for it?

When we complain about the church or refuse to get involved, what effect does it have?

What part do you think you should play in improving the church? Why?

4 BODY TALK

Explain that as members of the body of Christ (or the church), we all have different gifts and abilities to put to use.

Have volunteers read aloud I Corinthians 12:4-27. Point out that the letter of I Corinthians was written by Paul to a group of believers who were trying to understand what it means to "be a church." Paul gave them a very simple analogy—comparing the workings of the church to the workings of the human body—to aid their understanding.

Distribute copies of Student Sheet 11-B ("Body Talk") and pencils. Briefly explain the instructions for the sheet. Beside the different parts of the body, group members should write down gifts and abilities they have that correspond to those body parts. For example, next to the head someone might write "I'm smart" or "I think clearly." Next to the heart someone might write "I care about others" or "I can empathize with other people's emotions." Encourage group members to be honest about their gifts. Emphasize that this is not boasting—it is simply being honest about the talents God has given them.

Give them five minutes to list as many gifts and abilities as possible. When everyone is finished, ask volunteers to share some of the gifts and abilities they listed.

Say something like: **As the body of Christ, it is important for us to work together as a body—with each person performing specific functions. To do that, we must first understand ourselves and know our gifts and abilities. That takes time and practice. For now, though, what's one specific way you could use one of your abilities in our church? In this group?**

5 WE'RE ALL IN THIS TOGETHER

As you wrap up the session, emphasize that being part of the church means having to accept other members who are different from us—even though we may not understand these people or their value to the kingdom of God.

Say: **For example, old Mr. Henry always seems to be concerned with the financial "bottom line." He doesn't readily jump on the bandwagon when it comes to buying a new church van or pool table. If everyone were like him, the** church would have big problems. However, if he or someone like him weren't around, the problems would be equally as severe—the church would probably be bankrupt! So when people irritate you because they are different, don't forget that God can use their unique gifts to build the body of Christ.

Close the session in prayer, thanking God for the opportunity to be part of a church. Pray that each of your group members will learn more about his or her gifts and the importance he or she has in the church.

The Inventor's Plans

The inventor of the church, Jesus Christ, prayed about His invention nearly 2,000 years ago. Here are some of His goals for the church, mentioned in His prayer (quoted from John 17). After each statement, check off the "parts" of the invention that you think help accomplish that goal.

". . . That they [believers] may know you, the only true God, and Jesus Christ, whom you have sent . . ."

☐ Sermons   ☐ Youth group meetings   ☐ Small groups
☐ Singing   ☐ Sunday school classes   ☐ Helping poor people
☐ Social events   ☐ Offerings   ☐ Missions
☐ Drama   ☐ Communion   ☐ Other _____

PHIL. 3:10 ff

". . . That they may have the full measure of my joy within them . . ."

☐ Sermons   ☐ Youth group meetings   ☐ Small groups
☐ Singing   ☐ Sunday school classes   ☐ Helping poor people
☐ Social events   ☐ Offerings   ☐ Missions
☐ Drama   ☐ Communion   ☐ Other _____

Rom. 15:13

"As you sent me into the world, I have sent them into the world . . ."

☐ Sermons   ☐ Youth group meetings   ☐ Small groups
☐ Singing   ☐ Sunday school classes   ☐ Helping poor people
☐ Social events   ☐ Offerings   ☐ Missions
☐ Drama   ☐ Communion   ☐ Other _____

II COR. 5:17-20

" . . . May they also be in us [living close to the Lord] so that the world may believe that you have sent me."

☐ Sermons   ☐ Youth group meetings   ☐ Small groups
☐ Singing   ☐ Sunday school classes   ☐ Helping poor people
☐ Social events   ☐ Offerings   ☐ Missions
☐ Drama   ☐ Communion   ☐ Other _____

Phil. 2: 12-16

". . . That they may be one as we are one. . . . May they be brought to complete unity to let the world know that you sent me . . ."

☐ Sermons   ☐ Youth group meetings   ☐ Small groups
☐ Singing   ☐ Sunday school classes   ☐ Helping poor people
☐ Social events   ☐ Offerings   ☐ Missions
☐ Drama   ☐ Communion   ☐ Other _____

Eph. 4:1-3

Body Talk

"Just as each of us has one body with many members, and these members do not all have the same function, so in Christ we who are many form one body, and each member belongs to all the others" (Romans 12:4, 5).

Next to the body parts below, write down some of the talents, abilities, and characteristics you possess that relate to those body parts. (For instance, next to the elbow you might write "I am flexible.")

_____ Head

_____ Mouth

Eye _____

Ear _____

Arm _____

Hand _____

_____ Elbow

Heart _____

_____ Knee

Leg _____

Toe _____

_____ Foot

Session 12

Let's say you've clearly presented the Gospel to your youth group. Many of your kids have entered a personal relationship with Jesus Christ. However, you suspect that many of them feel that their journey of faith has *ended* in conversion instead of just beginning. Now comes the awesome task of helping kids recognize the need for continual Christian growth.

Without growth in the areas of prayer, Bible study, fellowship, service, and worship, young Christians go nowhere. And they're dangerously vulnerable to the influences of the world. A growing relationship with Jesus Christ brings us new life, new hope, and new challenges. We are never finished growing in Christ.

HOW DO I GROW AS A CHRISTIAN?

Specific Aims

• To help kids understand the importance of growing in Christ and becoming more spiritually mature; and to help kids understand that Bible study, prayer, fellowship with other believers, service, and witnessing are keys to Christian growth.

Scriptural Support

• Matthew 4:18-22; 16:13-19; 17:1-8
• Luke 5:1-11
• John 18:15-27; 21:15-19
• Acts 2:14-41

Special Preparation

• Bibles
• Copies of Student Sheet 12-A ("John and Kara: A Love Story")
• Copies of Student Sheet 12-B ("Now and Later")
• Pencils
• Chalkboard and chalk or newsprint and marker
• Paper
• Five keys labeled according to the instructions in Step 4 (optional)

1 A LOVE STORY?

Before the session, ask for three volunteers to participate in a skit. You'll need at least one guy and one girl for the skit. The third person may be either sex. Distribute a copy of Student Sheet 12-A ("John and Kara: A Love Story") to each volunteer. Assign the roles of John, Kara, and the narrator. Explain that as the narrator reads the skit, John and Kara must act it out. Give your volunteers a few minutes to read through the skit and plan what they want to do.

To begin the session, say something like: **Today we're going to open our session with one of the greatest love stories of all time.**

Introduce your actors and have them perform the skit. Afterward, lead the group in a round of applause.

Ask: **On a scale of one to ten, how would you rate this love story? Why?**

What's the problem with John and Kara's relationship? (They don't spend time with each other; they barely know each other.)

Do you think it's possible to truly love someone that you don't spend any time with? You may want to suggest that while it may be possible to have feelings of love for someone you barely know, you can't truly love that person for who he or she is unless you get to know the person—and getting to know the person requires time spent together.

2 WHAT'S IN A RELATIONSHIP?

Pass out paper and pencils.

Ask: **How many of you would say you love Christ? If you'd say that, draw a heart shape on your paper. Write your initials and "plus J. C." on the heart, as if you were carving it on a tree.**

Now, how many of you would say you have a relationship with Christ? If you'd say that, draw two dots on your paper to show how close that relationship is.

What does it mean to have a relationship with Christ? If someone suggests that having a relationship with Christ means believing in Him or asking Him into your heart, point out that that's simply the *beginning* of a relationship with Christ.

Have someone read aloud Matthew 4:18-22.

Say something like: **Having a relationship with Christ includes following Him. For the disciples mentioned in this passage, what did following Christ include?** (Immediately leaving everything behind and physically going wherever He went.)

Since Jesus is not physically present in the world now, how can we follow Him today? (By making our relationship with Him the most important thing in our lives and by living our lives according to His will.)

3 A LIFELONG RELATIONSHIP

During this step, to emphasize the idea of following Jesus, keep moving from one side of your meeting place to another. Kids should follow you each time you move, crowding on one side or the other. You could even walk in a circle and have kids follow you. Pause when they need to look up verses.

Say something like: **As we talk about a relationship with Christ, one of the best models for us to look at is the relationship the apostle Peter had with the Lord.**

Have someone read aloud Luke 5:1-11.

Ask: **How did Peter respond when the Lord asked Peter to follow Him?** (Peter left everything immediately and followed Him.) Compare Peter's response in this passage to the feelings many people have when they initially accept Christ as Savior. Peter was "on fire" in his faith, willing to follow the Lord anywhere. Likewise, new Christians are often very excited about their new faith and are eager to begin living their lives accordingly.

Have someone read aloud Matthew 16:13-19.

Say: **At this point Peter had been with Jesus for almost three years. What does that tell you about Peter's description of Him as "the Christ, the Son of the living God"?** (Peter wasn't making a hasty conclusion here. His confession was based on three years of following Jesus and listening to His teaching.) Point out that the more time we spend with Jesus—in prayer and in His Word—the more fully we'll be able to understand who He is, what He's done, and what He'll continue to do.

Have someone read aloud Matthew 17:1-8.

Ask: **If you were Peter, how would you feel about being allowed to witness such an incredible event?** (Honored, perhaps unworthy.) Point out that this was a "mountaintop" (no pun intended) spiritual experience for Peter, a high point in his relationship with Jesus. As we grow in our relationship with Christ, we too will have mountaintop experiences—times when we're rewarded for our faithfulness.

Have volunteers read aloud John 18:15-27.

Ask: **How do you think Peter felt after he'd denied Christ?** (Bitterly disappointed in himself, ashamed, perhaps as though he'd thrown away a relationship that took years to build.) Point out that Peter's experience demonstrates that no matter how strong our relationship is with the Lord or how long we've been developing it, we are never immune to setbacks and temptations.

Explain that Jesus forgave Peter for his denial and told Peter to keep serving Him in John 21:15-19.

Have group members quickly scan Acts 2:14-41. Explain that in this passage, Peter delivers one of the most powerful sermons about Jesus recorded in Scripture.

Ask: **What was the result of Peter's sermon in this passage?** (About three thousand people became Christians.) Point out that despite Peter's earlier (and later) failings, the Lord used him in a powerful way to spread the Gospel to thousands of people. The key was that Peter didn't allow his failing to destroy his relationship with Christ—he worked to rebuild it and continue in his spiritual growth.

Say: **Peter is an example of someone who continued to grow in faith. Like Peter, we are never finished growing spiritually.**

Let kids take their original seats before proceeding to the next step.

4 FIVE KEYS

Say something like: **Let's look at five keys to spiritual growth: Bible study, prayer, fellowship with other believers, service to others, and witnessing.** Write the keys on the board as you name them.

Have group members form five teams (or work individually if the group is small). Assign each team one of the keys. As a reminder, you could give the leader of each team a real key labeled with the letter B, P, F, S, or W. Instruct each team to answer this question: **How might your assigned key be helpful in a person's growing relationship with Christ?** For the sake of brevity, instruct each team to keep its answer to twenty-five words or less.

Give the teams a few minutes to work. When everyone is finished, ask each team to share its response.

Use the following suggestions (which are longer than twenty-five words) to supplement the teams' responses.

Bible study—The Bible outlines for us what it means to be a follower of Christ and what is involved in a relationship with Him. When we study God's Word, we equip ourselves to advance in our relationship with Christ.

Prayer—The best way to build a relationship with the Lord is to communicate with Him directly—telling Him how we feel about Him and asking for His guidance in our lives.

Fellowship with other believers—Jesus has given us the resource of other believers to assist us in developing our relationship with Him. Other believers can offer us advice, encourage us, and pray for us as we mature in our faith.

Service to others—The impact of your relationship with Jesus will spill over into all areas of your life, including your relationships with others. The better you know Christ, the more likely you are to follow His example of reaching out to and helping others.

Witnessing—Jesus commands His followers to tell others about Him. To do this, you first have to know enough about Him to tell others. The more you get to know Christ, the more you'll want to tell others about Him.

5 GETTING A LITTLE PERSONAL

Ask: **What's your personal relationship with the Lord like? Is it constantly growing, maturing, and developing? Or is it at a standstill? The best way to judge is to evaluate yourself in the five key areas on the board.**

Distribute copies of Student Sheet 12-B ("Now and Later"). Have group members complete the sentences in the first column to show where they are now in the five key areas for spiritual growth.

In the second column, have them complete the same sentences to show what they'd like to accomplish in the next year.

When everyone is finished, ask volunteers to share some of their responses. If time allows, have kids set specific one-year goals in each area. Let the group brainstorm steps needed to accomplish each goal. For instance, let's say Bob tells you that right now he shares his faith only if he's asked about it; in a year, he'd like to share his faith with at least one person a week. Your group might suggest that Bob read some how-to books on evangelism, take a personal evangelism class offered by your church, practice telling his story to another group member, etc.

After several volunteers have shared, wrap up the session by emphasizing again the importance of continuous growth in the Christian life.

Close the session in prayer.

JOHN AND KARA: A LOVE STORY

When John and Kara first passed each other in that dusty hallway at school, it was love at first sight. At first, Kara pretended not to notice John because she was afraid her friends might tease her. But as she was pretending to ignore him, she walked right into the drinking fountain, badly bruising her hip.

All morning John racked his brain, trying to think of some way to introduce himself to Kara. Finally, at lunch, he gathered his courage. With his tray in his hand, he approached Kara's table.

But when he got there and set down his tray, his mind went blank. He desperately searched for something to say. Finally, he blurted out the first words that popped into his mind: "My Jell-O used to live in Montana." John was horrified. But Kara quickly put him at ease with her bright laugh. It was an unusual beginning to a great relationship.

Kara and John never really dated in high school. He was always busy with football and basketball; she was a cheerleader and president of the Spanish club. However, they constantly thought about each other. They even refused to date other people because of their love and commitment. At least once a day, John would dial Kara's number. But he would hang up before she answered because he really didn't know what to say. Kara wrote John several letters, but didn't mail them because of her busy schedule.

But their love was true! At graduation, they gave each other a congratulatory hug after the ceremony. Again, they knew that they could never live without each other.

They went to different colleges, in different states, and never stopped thinking of each other. When someone would ask Kara out for a date, she would lower her eyes and say, "I'm sorry, my heart belongs to another." John was equally faithful. However, neither of them called, wrote, or visited the other. They couldn't stand the thought of living without each other.

Finally, after their junior years at college, John made his first phone call to Kara. "Will you marry me?" he asked in a trembling voice.

"Yes!" Kara screamed into the phone. "I love you!"

"I love you too," John said. "Let's get married now!" And so they did.

After the wedding reception, John and Kara got ready to leave. Through the rice and birdseed being thrown by the crowd they ran, holding hands.

"John," Kara said, "this has been the most beautiful day of my life. Let's get together again this time next year to celebrate our first anniversary."

"Oh, Kara, I would love to. Where will you be living during the year?"

"Chicago. And you?"

"Atlanta. Listen, call me if you ever need anything. You know how deeply I love you."

Kara gave him a hug. "And you, too, John. I'll always be true to you. I can hardly wait until next year. Take care!"

And with this final hug, Kara jumped into her car, John jumped into his, and they sped off.

"Wow, what a woman!" John said to himself.

"What a man!" Kara said to herself.

NOW AND LATER

In the first column, complete each sentence to show where you are now in each of the following areas. In the second column, complete the same sentences to show where you would like to be a year from now in each area.

	Now	*A Year from Now*
Bible Study • When I think about reading the Bible . . . • When I see my Bible . . . • When I try to read the Bible on my own . . . • After I read something in the Bible that I know I should do . . .		
PRAYER • When I pray, God probably . . . • When I'm worried, I . . . • When I'm really happy, I . . . • Praying aloud in a group . . .		
Fellowship with Other Believers • People in this group . . . • When I think about coming to church . . . • Reaching out to Christians I don't know . . . • After I've spent time with other Christians . . .		
Service to Others • The idea of me serving others . . . • When I think of other people's needs . . . • My favorite way to help people . . . • When I think of Jesus' service to me . . .		
Witnessing • My friends and Jesus . . . • When I think about sharing my faith . . . • The number of kids who know I'm a Christian . . . • My own story of coming to know Jesus . . .		

Session 13

What should kids do when they "don't know the basics"? Why, they should read the Bible! So all you have to do is tell them to study the Bible on their own, and you'll solve the problem. Right?

Wrong.

Sometimes we forget that for centuries only "experts" were permitted to read and interpret the Bible. Increasing literacy and the printing press helped change that, but the average person still needs assistance to get the most out of Scripture reading. That goes double for teenagers, and triple for kids who haven't spent much time in church.

This session won't make Bible scholars out of your young people. But it can introduce them to the idea of personal Bible study, and point out some helps to make the whole vital process easier.

THE WHY AND HOW OF BIBLE STUDY

Specific Aims

• To give kids the tools for building knowledge and faith through consistent, personal Bible study; and to provide kids with several different models of Bible study with which to experiment.

Scriptural Support

• II Timothy 3:16, 17

Special Preparation

• Bibles
• Copies of Student Sheet 13-A ("Quiz Time")
• Copies of Student Sheet 13-B ("Take Your Pick")
• Pencils
• Two volunteers dressed as bodyguards (see Step 1)
• Two paper bags filled with wood scraps and tools (see Step 2)
• Road map
• Encyclopedia volume
• Recipe book
• Phone book with Yellow Pages
• Various Bible study helps (see Step 4)

1 ANY QUESTIONS?

Before the session, get a couple of adults or group members to dress up as your "bodyguards" (with sunglasses, uniforms or sweatshirts and jeans, menacing expressions, and perhaps toy guns in holsters). Have your bodyguards stand beside you as you open the meeting. They should look as if they're ready to enforce what you say.

Make the following announcement: **From now on, every member of this group will see things my way. Based on my interpretations of the Bible, you will follow these rules:**

1. Because Adam was created before Eve, no girl may enter the room until all the guys have entered.

2. Because the Flood lasted forty days and forty nights, each of you must pay me forty cents each week.

3. Because Jonah was swallowed by a great fish, each of you must swallow a live goldfish at the end of this meeting.

4. Because the apostle Paul never ate a cheeseburger, you may never eat one either. The following foods are also off limits because they are not mentioned in the Bible: pizza, ice cream, potato chips, and chocolate.

5. Because Matthew 10:10 contains the phrase, "take no . . . sandals," you must take off your shoes and give them to my bodyguards—right now.

Some kids may comply; others may not. After seeing what happens, ask: **What do you think of my rules?**

Why won't you just do whatever I tell you, if I say it's based on the Bible?

How do you know whether something is really a Bible-based teaching or not?

As needed, point out that most of us aren't willing to blindly follow other people just because they quote the Bible. We want to think for ourselves.

Say: **That's just one reason to read the Bible for yourself—to decide whether to believe what you hear in church and from other people. What are some other reasons to read the Bible on your own?** (To find out how God, our Creator, wants us to live; to help us make better decisions; to know more about what God is like; to better understand ourselves and the world; etc.)

After talking about several reasons, thank your bodyguards and dismiss them (or just have them sit down, if they're group members).

2 HAVING THE RIGHT TOOLS

Before the session, you'll need to prepare two paper bags. In one bag, place several wood scraps, a hammer, nails, and sandpaper. In the other bag, place just wood scraps and nails.

Have group members form two teams. Give each team one of the bags. Announce that the teams have five minutes to create as many useful items as they can, using just the equipment in their bags.

Say: **Ready, go!** When the members of the second team open their bag and discover that they don't have any tools, they'll probably complain. Simply encourage them to work with what they have. They must not use the other team's tools. After five minutes, have each team display and explain its creations.

Afterward, say something like: **Of course, this activity wasn't fair. One team didn't have the necessary tools to work with. It's difficult—and sometimes even impossible—to accomplish something without the necessary tools.**

Have group members form four teams. Give Team #1 a local road map; give Team #2 an encyclopedia volume; give Team #3 a recipe book; and give Team #4 a phone book (with a Yellow Pages or business section).

Before the session, prepare an assignment for each team, based on the team's resource.

For instance, depending on the specific resources used, you might give the following assignments.

Team #1—Find the approximate distance between our town and the state capital.

Team #2—Find out how many years Abraham Lincoln lived in Kentucky.

Team #3—Find out how many eggs are needed for angel food cake.

Team #4—Find the telephone number of the pizza place with the shortest name in the book.

The team that completes its assignment first wins.

Afterward, discuss which team had the most difficult assignment and which team's resource was easiest to use.

Then say: **Today we're going to be talking about a very important assignment—understanding the Bible—and we're going to be looking at tools and resources designed to help us with this assignment.**

3 UNDERSTANDING THE WORLD'S MOST IMPORTANT BOOK

Ask: **On a scale of one to ten, with one being "very easy" and ten being "almost impossible," how hard is it for you to study the Bible?** Emphasize that you're not talking about finding the time to study the Bible; you're talking about understanding what the Bible says and getting something from it. Encourage all of your group members to respond and to explain their responses.

Ask: **What's difficult about studying the Bible?** (The language is hard to understand; it's boring; some parts don't seem to make sense; I don't see what it has to do with my life today; etc.)

What would make Bible study easier for you? (Having someone tell me what certain passages are talking about; being able to understand some of the strange wording and phrases; being able to recognize how it applies to my life today; etc.)

Point out that Bible study is one of the ways we grow in our relationship with Christ. Therefore, it's important that we find a way to do it.

4 TOOLS OF THE TRADE

One at a time, hold up various Bible study aids (Bible dictionary, Bible concordance, biblical reference book, Bible atlas, devotional guide, paraphrased translation of the Bible, etc.). Briefly explain the purpose of each. Use the following information to supplement your explanations.

Bible dictionary—A reference book that explains the meaning of words and gives background information on them.

Bible concordance—A resource that allows you to find Scripture references using key words found in the passage. (Many Bibles have a concordance in the back of them.)

Biblical reference book—Any nonfiction book that provides insight into Scripture.

Bible atlas—A collection of maps and other geographical information pertaining to biblical times and events.

Devotional guide—A nonreference book (or booklet) designed to teach some inspirational truth about a biblical principle.

Paraphrased translation of the Bible—An easy-to-understand version of the Bible based on English translations and not necessarily on the original languages of Greek and Hebrew.

Say: **Now let's do a quick exercise to put some of the resources to use.**

Distribute copies of Student Sheet 13-A ("Quiz Time") and pencils. Set out all of the Bible study aids in front of the group. Explain that the group must use the resources to complete the quiz. As needed, encourage kids to use the Bible's upfront index to find books of the Bible.

Give group members several minutes to work. When everyone is finished, go over the correct answers as a group.

The correct answers are as follows:

(1) Money

(2) Seventy miles

(3) Hebrews 13:8

(4) Among the passages kids might mention: Psalm 46:9; Isaiah 2:4; and Micah 4:3

(5) A perfumed spice

(6) Luke 19

(7) Asher, Manasseh, and Dan

Point out that most of these study aids are probably available through your church library or even your local public library. While some of the aids (Bible dictionary, Bible concordance, Bible atlas) probably aren't necessary every time we read the Bible, they are handy when we have a question about a topic or when we want to explore a subject more deeply.

5 BLUEPRINTS FOR BIBLE STUDY

Say something like: **Not only are there resources available to help you study the Bible, but there are also different types of Bible study you can do, depending on what you're looking for.**

Distribute copies of Student Sheet 13-B ("Take Your Pick").

Give group members a few minutes to read about the three types of Bible study described on the sheet. Afterward, if you've used any of three methods in your own Bible study, describe your experiences. Explain which method you liked best and why. If you had struggles with one or more of the methods, share them as well.

Ask: **If you were going to begin a Bible study tomorrow, which of these three methods would you use? Why?** Encourage most of your group members to respond.

Then ask: **Do you think Bible study is something that should be done every day? If so, how much time do you think you should spend in the Bible every day?** After several group members have offered their opinions, suggest that while Bible study should become a regular practice, setting unrealistic goals for Bible study quickly leads to frustration. Suggest that fifteen minutes a day might be a good initial goal for Bible study.

[OPTION: If you have time, you might want to wrap up the session with a brief Bible study (which you've prepared beforehand) based on one of the three methods described on Student Sheet 13-B. If possible, it would be good to use some of the study aids (from Step 4) in this Bible study.]

Have someone read aloud II Timothy 3:16, 17. Then close the session in prayer, asking God to give your group members guidance and patience as they attempt to establish regular Bible study habits.

1. The King James Version of Matthew 6:24b says, "Ye cannot serve God and mammon." What is mammon?

_____

2. About how far was it from Cana, where Jesus turned water into wine at the wedding feast, to Bethany, where He raised Lazarus from the dead?

_____

3. "Jesus Christ is the same yesterday and today and forever." Where is this verse found in the Bible?

_____

4. Name three Bible passages in which a spear is mentioned.

_____
_____
_____

5. Matthew 2:11 tells us that the Magi presented the baby Jesus with gold, incense, and myrrh. What is myrrh?

_____

6. In what chapter of the Bible is Zacchaeus mentioned?

_____

7. Of the twelve tribes of Israel, name three whose land bordered the Great (Mediterranean) Sea.

_____
_____

Take Your Pick

Verse-by-Verse Study

How it works: You pick a book or extended passage of the Bible and explore it, literally, verse by verse. Each verse is studied in the context of the rest of the book or passage. Rather than study a verse by itself, you study how that verse relates to other truths found in the book.

Benefits: This method gives you the "big picture" of the book or passage you're studying, instead of just "snippets" of insight here and there. It also allows you to study some of the lesser-known parts of the Bible.

Drawbacks: This method takes a lot of time to complete. Depending on the size of the book or passage, it may take you months. Also, some of the passages you come across in a verse-by-verse study may not be as exciting or informative as you'd like. A Bible commentary can help explain tough verses, though.

One of the best passages for a verse-by-verse study is the Book of James.

Topical Study

How it works: You choose a subject that you'd like to learn more about and explore passages in the Bible related to that subject. For example, if you chose "sin" as a topic, you would explore verses that talk about sin and its results. You would also explore the lives of people in the Bible who sinned. You'd try to discover what they did—or didn't do—about their sins.

Depending on how deep you want to get, a topical study might also involve researching the meaning of words in their original forms, comparing related passages, and consulting other sources (a Bible encyclopedia, for instance) to learn more.

Benefit: This method allows you to get a detailed overview of a topic of interest to you.

Drawback: This method takes time and work to research all the passages relating to a topic.

Devotional Study

How it works: Devotional Bible study gives you inspiration, encouragement, and guidance. You'd usually try to use it to find a truth to apply immediately to your life. For instance, if you were facing a big decision, you might look for one or two verses on wisdom to help you. Or if you were feeling lonely, you might look for a few verses on loneliness.

Benefits: This method helps you focus on God's presence in your daily activities. Also, devotional studies usually take less time than the other two methods.

Drawback: This method tends to be "surface," and doesn't really allow for in-depth study.

Session 14

When kids don't know the basics of the Christian life, they aren't likely to know much about prayer. They may think of prayer as something you do in an emergency—even though it may not do any good. They may put non-emergency praying in the same dull, sedentary "little old lady" category as knitting and quilting.

Prayer is more powerful than we can measure. Yet the basics of prayer are easy enough for nearly anyone to understand: Prayer is talking with God. This session should give your kids the "basic training" they need to start trying this form of communication with their Creator.

THE WHY AND HOW OF PRAYER

Specific Aims

• To help kids recognize that prayer is simply talking with and listening to God; to help them understand that we gain great strength through prayer; and to help them understand the importance of continuous prayer (as opposed to "crisis" praying).

Scriptural Support

• Psalms 5:1-7; 8:1-9; 25:1-7; 32:1-11; 34:1-7; 51:1-17; 61:1-4; 62:1-8; 98:1-9; 103:1-5
• I John 5:14

Special Preparation

• Bibles
• Cut-apart copy of Student Sheet 14-A ("A Message to Send")
• Copies of Student Sheet 14-B ("What Are Your Motives?")
• Pencils
• Chalkboard and chalk or newsprint and marker
• Paper

1 IMPAIRED COMMUNICATION

Before the session, cut apart a copy of Student Sheet 14-A ("A Message to Send") to form fifteen cards. As group members arrive, give each of them a card. They may not show anyone else what is on their cards.

Say: **You have five minutes to get someone else in the group to guess what's on your card. However, as you give clues, you may not say, draw, or write anything. Ready, go!**

Probably few, if any, of your group members will have their messages guessed.

After five minutes, ask: **What was the biggest obstacle you faced in trying to get others to guess your message?** (Not being able to talk, draw, or write.)

How would our relationships be different if we couldn't communicate with each other? (We wouldn't be able to share our joys and frustrations with each other; our relationships probably wouldn't be as close; etc.)

Do you ever wish you could communicate with God? Some kids may point out that they can, through prayer. Others may wish for a more face-to-face form of communication.

If God were on a radio call-in show, what kinds of questions do you think He might get? What would you like to ask or tell Him?

Say something like: **In this session we're going to be talking about the most important communication we have—one that many of us often forget about—prayer.** Point out that prayer is one of the most important aspects of the Christian life because it allows us to communicate *directly* with God.

2 SOMETHING'S COME BETWEEN US

Ask for four volunteers to participate in some "instant skits." You will assign each one of them a "prayer obstacle"—something that prevents people from praying. Each person will then act out what happens when someone can't seem to overcome that obstacle.

The obstacles are as follows:
- busyness—not having enough time to pray;
- speechlessness—not knowing what to say to God;
- poor timing—praying at poorly chosen times (that is, right before you fall asleep);
- misunderstanding—having wrong ideas about prayer (that is, that prayer is simply telling God what you want from Him, that prayers must be elaborate and include phrases like "Thou art sovereign," that prayer is only for emergencies, etc.).

For instance, the person assigned "busyness" might act out a scene in which a person tries to pray, but is constantly interrupted (by the telephone, other people, the television, his or her own stray thoughts, etc.).

Give volunteers about a minute to prepare; then have them present their roleplays. When all four of them are finished, lead the rest of the group in a round of applause.

3 A SOLUTION FOR EVERY OBSTACLE

Say something like: **Now that we've identified some of the obstacles to prayer, let's brainstorm some ways to overcome those obstacles. The first obstacle we mentioned was "busyness—not having enough time to pray."**

Open your Bible and pretend you are reading the following from it: **"A person shall be judged by the length of his prayer. He who speaks many words at a time to the Lord shall be blessed. Do not dishonor your heavenly Father by praying but for a minute."**

Ask: **In which book of the Bible can this passage be found?** Many of your group members may recognize that it's not from the Bible.

Emphasize that the Bible does not say we have to set aside long blocks of time for prayer. Praying for five minutes in the car on the way to school or for ten minutes as you work out is a good way to begin a regular prayer habit.

Say: **The second obstacle we mentioned was "speechlessness—not knowing what to say to God."**

Which of the following do you think is important to God? Stand up if you think the item I read is important to Him.

(a) your request for forgiveness for a sin you've committed

(b) your gratitude for something He's done for you

(c) your need for guidance in making a major decision about your future

(d) your romantic feelings for the person of the opposite sex you met last week

Point out that God has a personal interest in *every* area of our lives. We can and should share with Him everything that's on our minds.

Say: **The third obstacle we mentioned was "poor timing—praying at poorly chosen times."** Draw a clock face with numbers on the board. Invite several kids to come up and shade in parts of the clock face to show their answers to the next question. **Besides right before falling asleep, when are some other poor times to pray?** (When you face constant interruptions, when your mind is on other things, etc.)

Point out that while it's not necessary to set aside long blocks of time to pray, it is necessary to set aside blocks of time that allow you to focus your full attention on God.

Say: **The fourth obstacle we identified was "misunderstanding—having wrong ideas about prayer." To overcome this obstacle, we need to examine what the Bible says prayer is—and what it isn't.**

4 The Psalms of Prayer

Write the following references from Psalms on the board. Have group members form pairs. Distribute paper and pencils to the pairs. Instruct each pair to look up as many passages as it can in five minutes and write down what each passage tells us about prayer.

Use the following information to supplement the pairs' responses.

• Psalm 5:1-7—Prayer is a time of simple honesty. We should tell the Lord exactly what's going on in our lives.

• Psalm 8:1-9—Prayer is a time of awe. We should reflect on the incredible things the Lord has done and tell Him how we feel about them.

• Psalm 25:1-7—Prayer is a time of forgiveness. We should confess our sins to God and expect Him never to remember them again.

• Psalm 32:1-11—Prayer is a time of instruction from God. Taking our requests to God is only part of the prayer process. We also need to be open to His leading as we listen and as we meditate on His Book.

• Psalm 34:1-7—Prayer is a time of praising God. We should tell God what we love and admire about Him.

• Psalm 51:1-17—Prayer is a time of confession. It is a time to admit our failings "face-to-face" with God.

• Psalm 61:1-4—Prayer is a time of drawing strength. When we haven't got the resources to continue, we can tap into God's strength.

• Psalm 62:1-8—Prayer can be a time of silence and rest. It doesn't always have to involve active conversation. Sometimes it might just involve sitting back and relaxing, knowing that we're loved and protected by God.

• Psalm 98:1-9—Prayer can be a time of laughter and joy. The Christian life is full of happiness and good times. They should be reflected in our prayers.

• Psalm 103:1-5—Prayer is a time of peace. When we're troubled, we can know that God will ease our minds.

5 Motives

Say something like: **Not everyone has a clear understanding of what prayer is. And misunderstandings often lead people to pray with the wrong motives. Some people use prayer for selfish reasons.**

Distribute copies of Student Sheet 14-B ("What Are Your Motives?") and pencils. Say: **Read through each of the situations described on the sheet. Decide whether you think each person's motive for praying is selfish or not.**

Give group members a few minutes to work. When everyone is finished, designate one side of the room as "selfish" and the other as "not selfish." Read the situations aloud and have group members take their places between one wall and the other to indicate how they responded.

Use the following information to supplement group members' responses.

(1) Harold's motive seems to be selfish. He wants God to just *give* him the car; he doesn't seem willing to do anything (other than "being good") to earn the car.

(2) Danise's motive doesn't seem selfish. She's asking God for His strength in overcoming a difficult situation.

(3) Juan's motive doesn't seem selfish. He's not asking for God's help out of laziness. After all, Juan has visited and studied several different colleges. He's asking God for wisdom and guidance in making his decision.

(4) Tina's motive seems selfish. She's asking for God's help out of laziness. She's put off investigating the colleges, so now she wants God to make the decision for her.

(5) Soo Li's motive doesn't seem selfish. She's thanking God for His handiwork.

(6) Jolene's motive doesn't seem selfish. She's asking God to help her make a decision about Him. But she also seems willing to put some effort into the process herself.

Have someone read aloud I John 5:14.

Ask: **According to this verse, what is the key to effective prayer?** (Asking according to God's will.)

What happens if we pray for something according to God's will? (We will receive what we ask for.)

How can we learn to pray according to God's will? If no one mentions it, suggest that we can pray for this kind of guidance too. God can and will help us learn to pray according to His will. It's also a matter of practice. The more we pray, the "better" we become at it (or the better we're able to recognize God's will).

As you wrap up the session, emphasize that prayer is more than asking God for things. Prayer is communication, a conversation between you and God. Conversation involves talking *and* listening.

Close the session with a time of silent prayer, giving kids the opportunity to put to use some of the prayer principles you talked about in the session.

A Message to Send

My favorite animal in the zoo is the rhinoceros.	Two days ago, a car splashed mud all over my new clothes.	I haven't brushed or flossed my teeth in a week.
I left my bowling ball in my locker at school.	Last night my little brother tried to eat my math homework.	My pet hamster was injured in a skydiving accident.
When I was little, I used to put rocks in my nose.	My grandmother plays guitar in a rock band.	This morning I got a phone call from the police.
My mother lost her boxing match last night.	I got lost in the frozen food section of the supermarket.	I saw a double feature at the drive-in last Friday.
I will not shake hands with anyone shorter than I am.	My fingers feel like they're going to fall off my hand.	My dog sent me a postcard from Hawaii last week.

WHAT ARE YOUR MOTIVES?

Read each of the following situations. Then decide whether the person's motive for praying is selfish or not.

1. Harold is crazy about cars! He reads *Hot Rod* and *Car* magazines almost all the time. "Dear God," he prays, "please help me get a red sports car. I promise I'll be good if You do!"

SELFISH   Not Selfish

2. Danise has just broken up with Sal. She sits in her room, crying, and prays, "God, it hurts so much! I don't know how I can face Sal tomorrow at school. Please give me strength."

SELFISH   Not Selfish

3. Juan is confused about college. He has studied many different schools and has visited three of them. But he still can't make up his mind. He whispers in prayer as he enters his high school counselor's office, "Please help me make the right decisions."

SELFISH   Not Selfish

4. Tina is also confused about college. She has procrastinated for weeks and hasn't read any of the material sent to her from the schools. Now it's time for her to decide. She spreads out a bunch of school catalogs on the floor, closes her eyes, and prays, "Lord, please let me choose the school that You want me to go to."

SELFISH   Not Selfish

5. Soo Li looks at the beautiful sunset with the hues of blue, purple, red, and orange. "Wow," she whispers, "that's beautiful! Thank You, God!"

SELFISH   Not Selfish

6. Jolene looks at the beautiful sunset with the hues of blue, purple, red, and orange. "You know, God," she whispers, "I don't know if You really exist or not, but that's beautiful! If You exist, please help me figure out what to believe."

SELFISH   Not Selfish

Session 15

Many Christian teens struggle with hard-to-overcome habits or lifestyles that didn't completely change when they accepted Christ. As a result, many of them feel as though they're "not good enough for God."

The closer we get to Christ, the more likely we are to be powerfully convicted by the Holy Spirit to confess sin and restore our relationship with Christ. This "conviction of sin" feels strangely like guilt. In fact, it is guilt. However, it is guilt that brings us to repentance and renewal, not depression and disillusionment. Kids need to know that God wants us to avoid sin for a reason—He doesn't want us to get hurt. And when we still choose to sin, God wants to help us through our mistakes. Sin is not to be taken lightly; nor is the fear of sin to be a controlling element in our lives.

I'M A CHRISTIAN, BUT I STILL SIN—WHAT CAN I DO ABOUT IT?

Specific Aims

• To help kids understand that becoming a Christian does not mean automatic perfection—we live in a sinful world and we still slip up and sin; and to help them understand that God forgives us when we sin—if we ask Him to.

Scriptural Support

• Psalm 103:12
• Isaiah 43:25
• Romans 12:2
• I John 1:8—2:1; 3:4-6

Special Preparation

• Bibles
• Copies of Student Sheet 15-A ("Half-Baked Headlines")
• Cut-apart copies of Student Sheet 15-B ("'I' Charts")
• Pencils
• Chalkboard and chalk or newsprint and marker
• Small plastic basketball hoop
• Two or three foam rubber basketballs
• Dictionary (optional) (see Step 1)

1 SO-CALLED EXPERTS

Before the session, set up a small plastic basketball hoop in your room. You'll also need to have two or three foam rubber basketballs.

To open the session, ask: **Do we have any basketball players in the room?** Explain that you're not necessarily asking for people who play on the varsity team—you're just looking for people who consider themselves basketball players. When your basketball players identify themselves, explain that they will be sitting out the first activity—but that you have something special planned for them later.

Have the rest of the group participate in a brief contest to see who can make the most "free throws" from a certain spot in the room.

When the game is over, say something like: **You guys did pretty well—for non-basketball players. But now we're going to watch some experts at work.**

Call each of your basketball players forward one at a time. Give him or her a ball and have him or her shoot free throws from the same place the rest of the group shot. When a basketball player misses a shot, act as though you're horrified. Say something like: **I thought you said you were a basketball player! You didn't even hit the shot! Next!** Before the person has a chance to respond, bring on the next basketball player. Continue this until all the basketball players have missed a shot.

Afterward, ask: **Is it possible to be a basketball player and still miss shots occasionally?** If no one mentions it, point out that the best players in the NBA usually hit only about 50 percent of their shots.

[NOTE: If you can't find a basketball hoop or if you know that few of your group members consider themselves basketball players, you might use a dictionary and ask how many group members consider themselves good spellers. Then you could hold a spelling bee for the rest of the group members. Afterward, you could bring on your "good spellers" to give a demonstration. When a good speller misspells a word, you would act horrified, as in the basketball example.]

2 THE CHRISTIAN AND THE THREE-LETTER WORD

Say something like: **OK, so it's possible for a person to call himself or herself a basketball player even though he or she misses some shots. Now let's think in terms of our spiritual lives. Is it possible for a person to be a Christian even though he or she occasionally does things that go against God and His Word?** Encourage several group members to offer their opinions.

Ask: **What three-letter word refers to acts that go against God and His Word?** (Sin.)

Do Christians sin? (Yes.)

How is it possible for a person who claims to follow the Lord to do things that go against Him and His Word? (Even though we're Christians, we still live in a sinful world and are still "tripped up" by our old selves.)

Refer back to the basketball illustration. Ask: **How does a basketball coach feel about missed shots?** (He may dislike them, but he knows his players aren't perfect and can't be expected to hit every shot.)

How do you think the Lord feels about Christians who struggle with sin? (He despises our sin—but because He loves us, He's ready and willing to help and forgive us. He knows that because of our nature and because we live in a sinful world, we're going to sin sometimes.) Emphasize that sin is never "OK" with God. Every time we sin, we put an obstacle in our relationship with the Lord. The obstacle remains there until we ask for forgiveness for the sin. Knowing that God forgives us does *not* give us license to continue sinning.

Have someone read aloud I John 3:4-6.

Ask: **Is this passage saying that if we commit a sin after we've accepted Christ as Savior, we can no longer be Christians?** (No. It's saying that when we become Christians, we are no longer slaves to sin. Because we're human, we'll still sin on occasion. But our lives are now characterized not by sin, but by doing what's right.)

Distribute copies of Student Sheet 15-A ("Half-Baked Headlines"). Let kids look the headlines over.

Ask: **What do these headlines have in common?** (They're about people who have the chance to be free, but won't take it. They choose to stay where they are.)

How are these people like Christian kids who keep sinning? (Christians have been set free from slavery to sin, but they often choose to obey their former "master" anyway.)

So what can we do about this?

Have a group member read aloud Romans 12:2.

Ask: **What does it mean to be conformed to this world?** (Living the same kind of lifestyle that non-Christians live.)

How does God change us from within? (He frees us from our slavery to sin; He gives us the resources to resist the temptation to sin.)

3 FORGIVENESS AND "FORGETNESS"

Have someone read aloud I John 1:8-10.

Ask: **According to verse 9, what should we do if we sin?** (Confess it to God.)

What happens when we confess a sin? (God forgives us and purifies us.)

What does it mean to be purified? (To be made clean.)

What limitations does verse 9 place on asking God for forgiveness? In other words, how often can we come to God with a sin to be forgiven before He says, "That's it. I've had enough. I'm not going to forgive any more of your sins"? If no one mentions it, point out the word "faithful." This refers to the fact that God can be *counted on* to forgive our sins any time we ask Him to—as long as we are truly sorry for what we've done and as long as we are actively committed to battling our sinful natures. There is no limit to the number of times God will forgive us.

Say something like: **I John 2:1 gives us an interesting look at what happens when we ask God for forgiveness.** Have someone look it up.

Ask: **What does this verse make you think of?** If no one mentions it, suggest that it resembles a courtroom scene. We are on trial for our sin; God is the judge; and Christ is our defense lawyer.

Ask: **What do you think Christ says to God the Father in our defense?** If no one mentions it, suggest that He might say something like this: "I took this person's sins upon Myself and paid the price. Do not hold him or her responsible for them any longer."

How does it make you feel to know that Christ is defending you before God? (Secure, grateful, relieved, responsible—not wanting to "abuse" the privilege, etc.)

Have volunteers read aloud Psalm 103:12 and Isaiah 43:25.

Ask: **What do these verses tell us about what happens to our sins after we've confessed them to God?** (They are removed from us completely and forgotten about, never to be brought up again.) Point out that this gives us the freedom to stop worrying about the things we've done in the past and allows us to focus our attention on living God-honoring lives *right now.* It does *not* give us the freedom to continue sinning.

4 I.O.U.

Before or during the session, cut the two "'I' Charts" from copies of Student Sheet 15-B. You'll need a pair of charts for each group member.

At this point in the session, give each person a pair of charts. Form pairs. Have partners take turns giving each other "eye exams" by seeing how far away they can stand from each other and still read each chart aloud.

Then ask: **Why is it sometimes hard for us to "see" the facts that are printed on these two charts?** (We feel guilty about what we've done wrong; the devil keeps accusing us; some sins seem more attractive than obeying God; etc.)

As a group, read the charts aloud. Encourage kids to take the charts home as reminders of their freedom in Christ. Then close in prayer.

Millionaire Sweepstakes Winner Keeps
His Job as a Pizza Delivery Man

Slaves Tell President Lincoln, "We Don't Want to Be Free!"

Former Cocaine Addict
Kicks Habit, Becomes
Alcoholic Instead

High School Graduate Volunteers to Take
All Her Classes "One More Time"

Hostage Freed; Decides to
Stay in Basement Dungeon

Released from Prison after 20 Years, Man Refuses to Leave

Lazarus, Raised from Dead,
Won't Come Out of His Tomb

I O U

EVERYTHING,

LORD JESUS, FOR

WIPING OUT MY SINS AND

FOR DEFENDING ME BEFORE YOUR

FATHER. THANK YOU FOR MAKING IT POSSIBLE

FOR MY SINS TO BE GONE FOREVER.

I O U

NOTHING,

YOU OLD LIAR, THE

DEVIL. CHRIST HAS SET ME

FREE, BREAKING THE CHAINS THAT

USED TO HOLD ME AND MAKING IT POSSIBLE

FOR ME TO HAVE ETERNAL LIFE.